beloved maidens

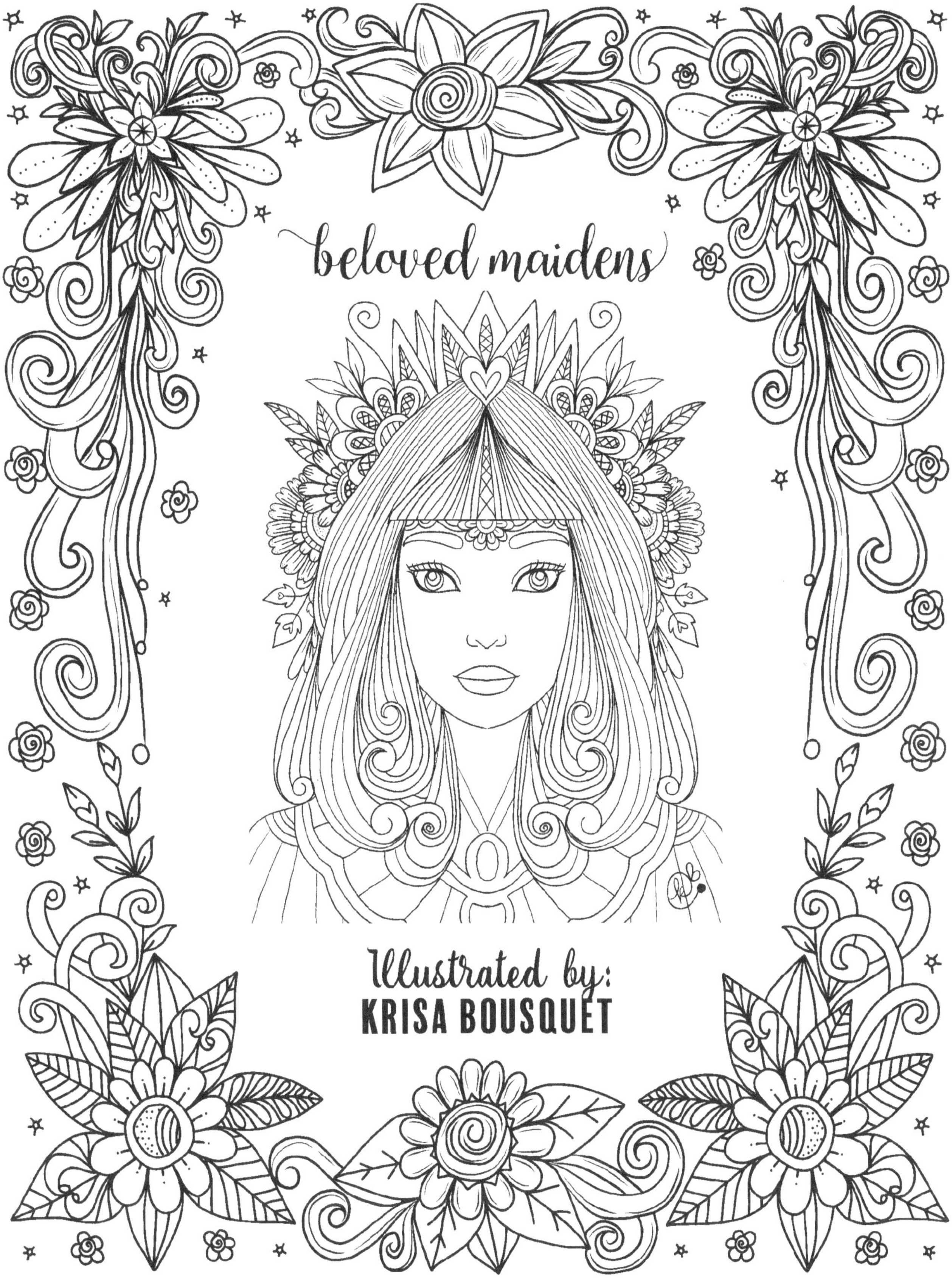

Illustrated by:
KRISA BOUSQUET

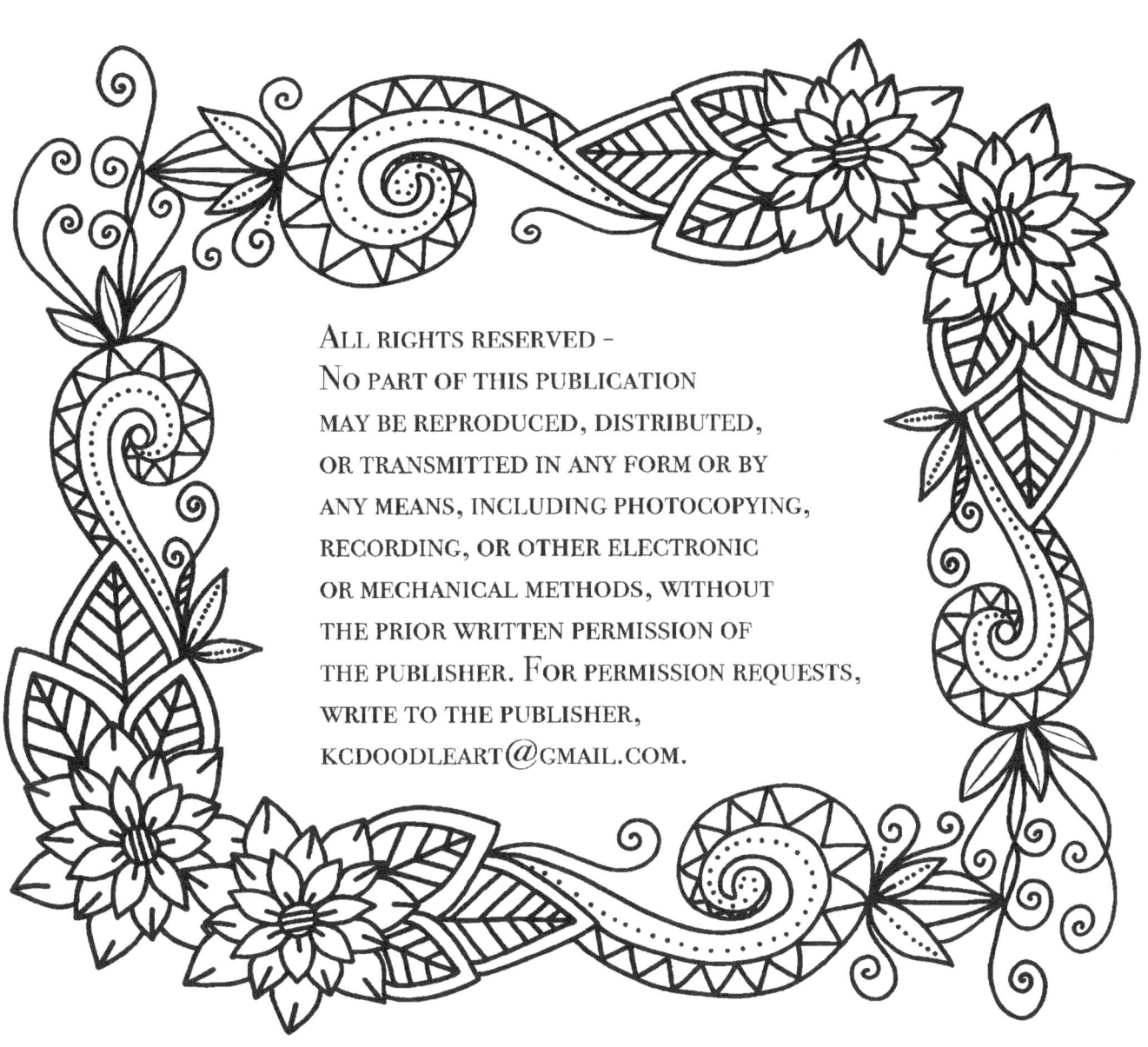

All rights reserved -
No part of this publication
may be reproduced, distributed,
or transmitted in any form or by
any means, including photocopying,
recording, or other electronic
or mechanical methods, without
the prior written permission of
the publisher. For permission requests,
write to the publisher,
kcdoodleart@gmail.com.

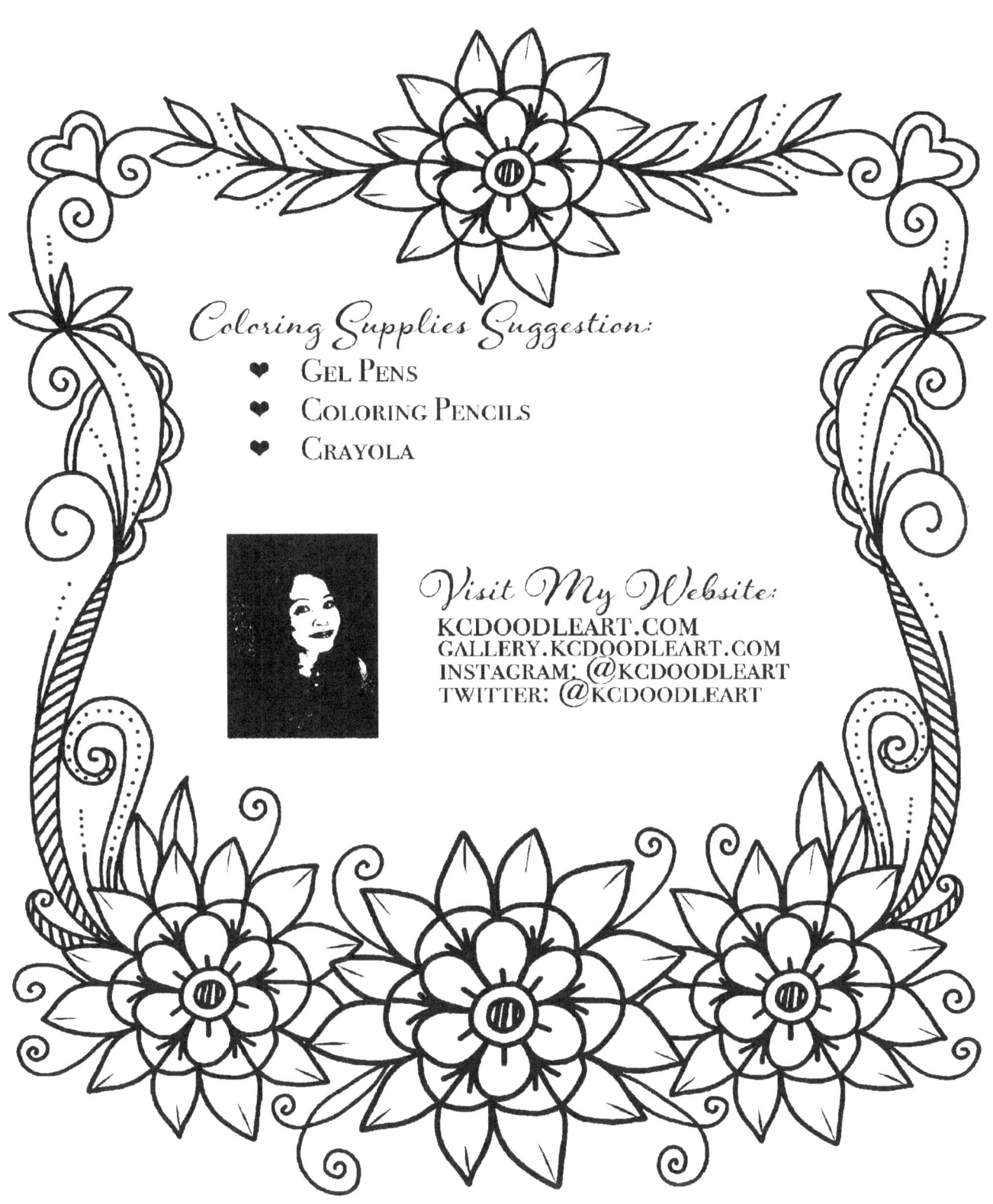

this Book Belongs To:

_____

_____

_____

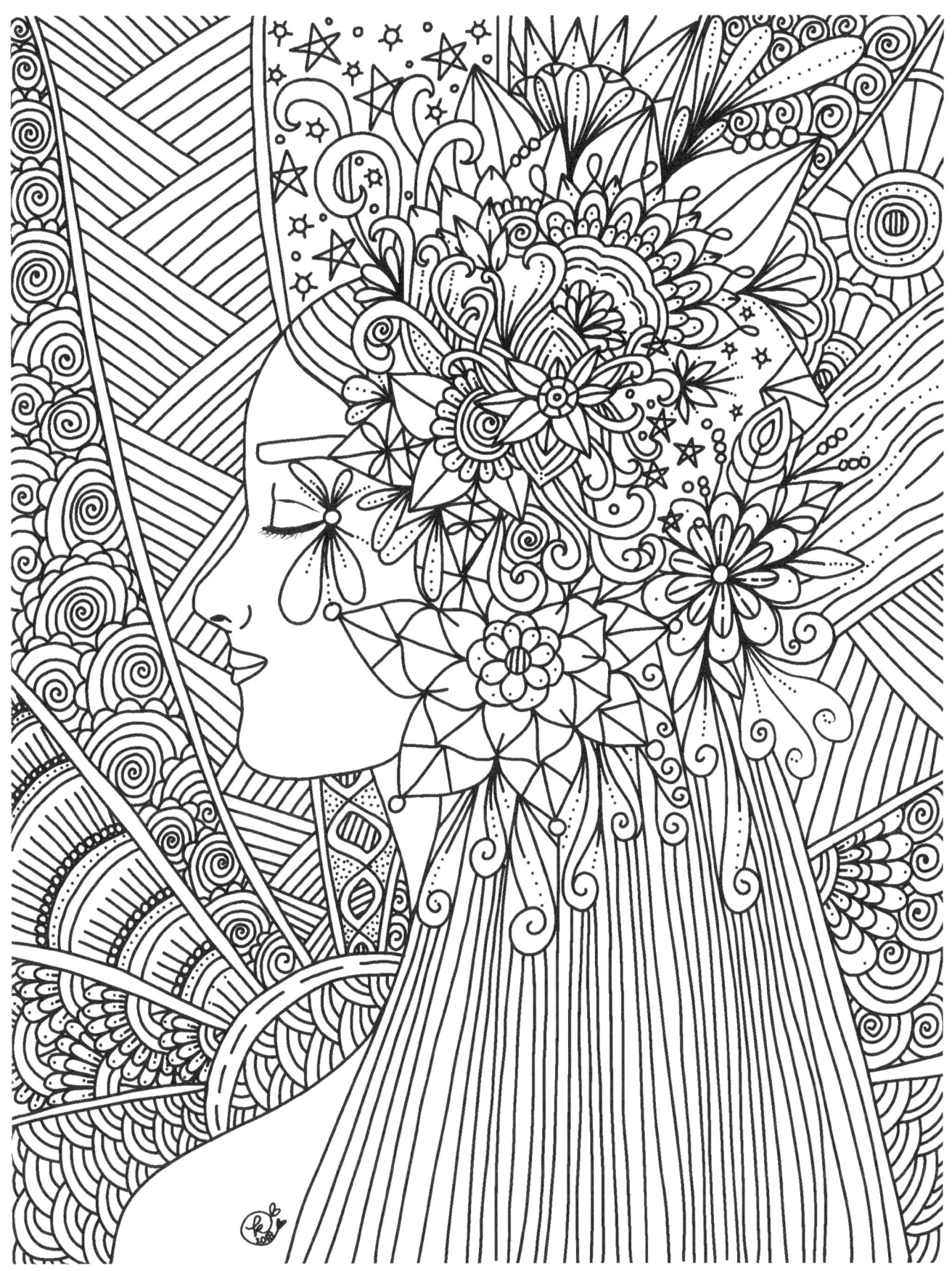

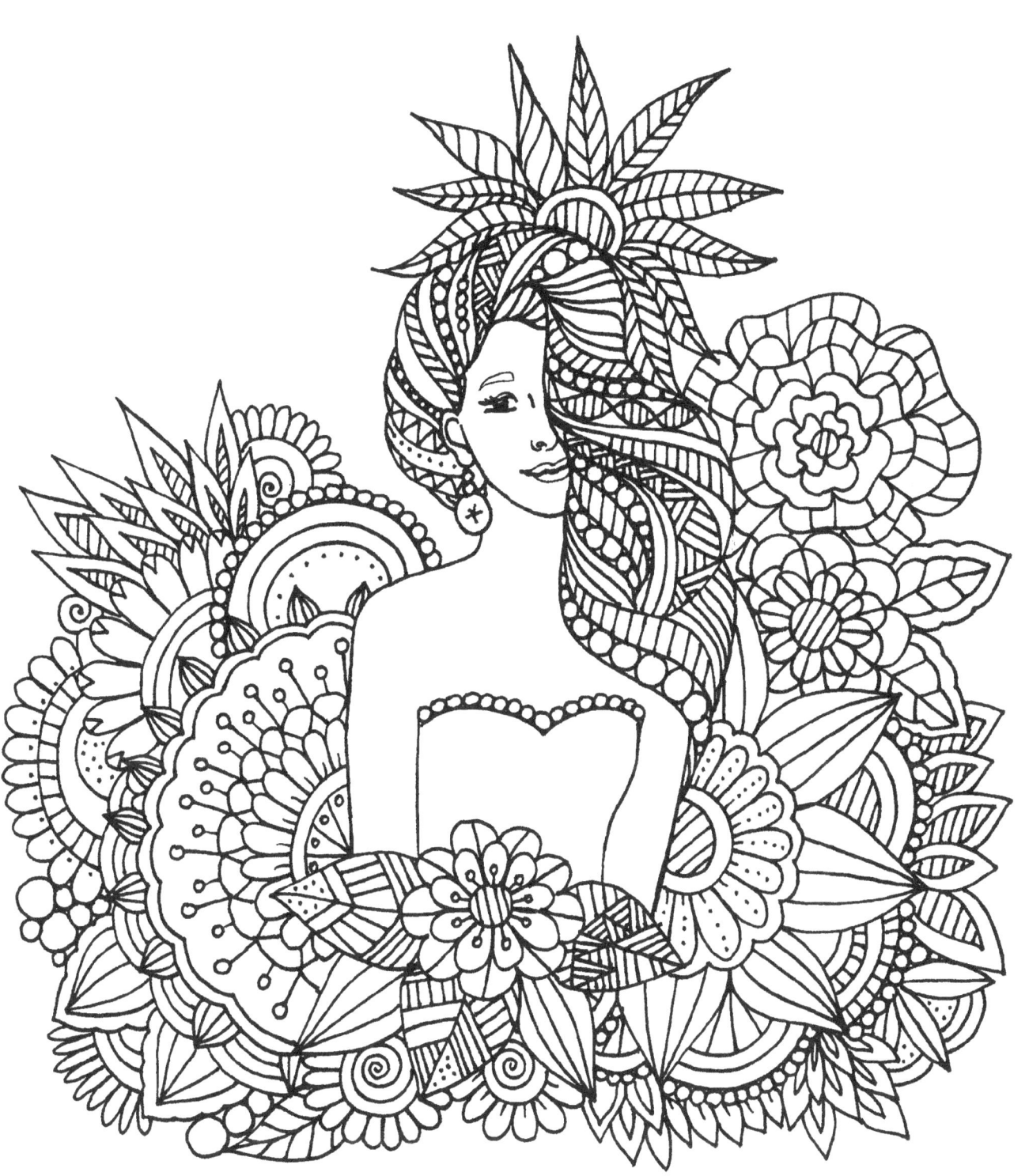

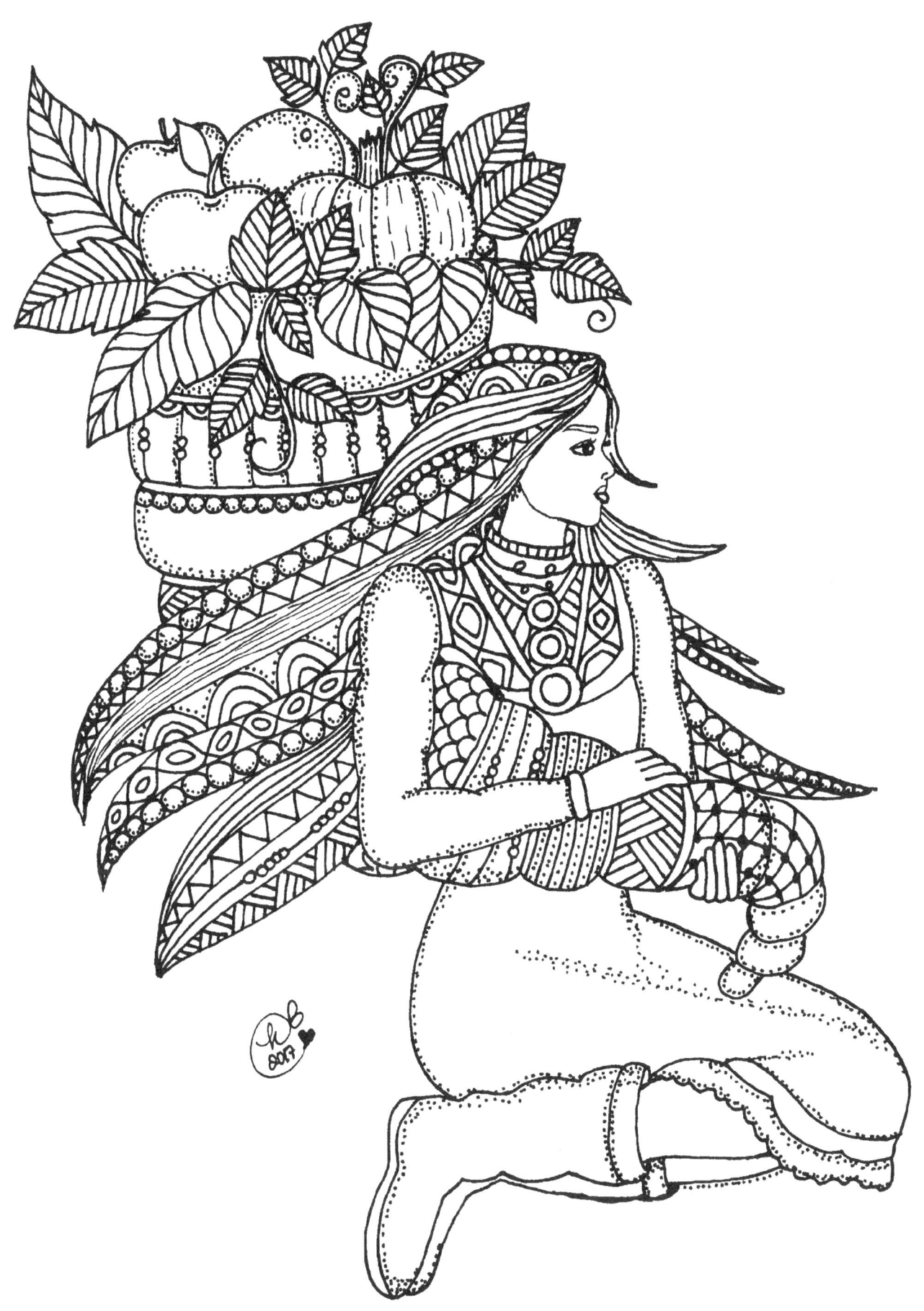

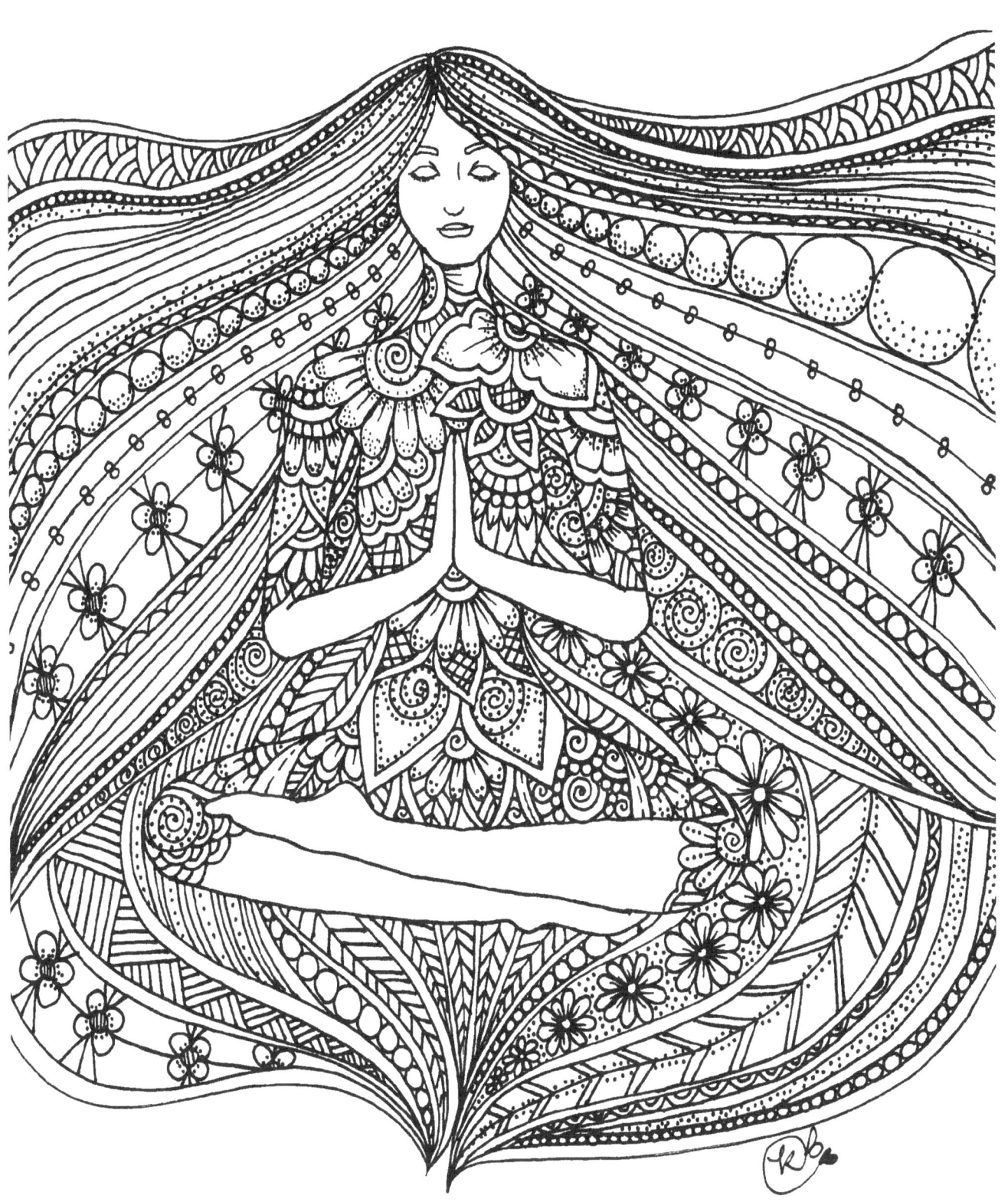

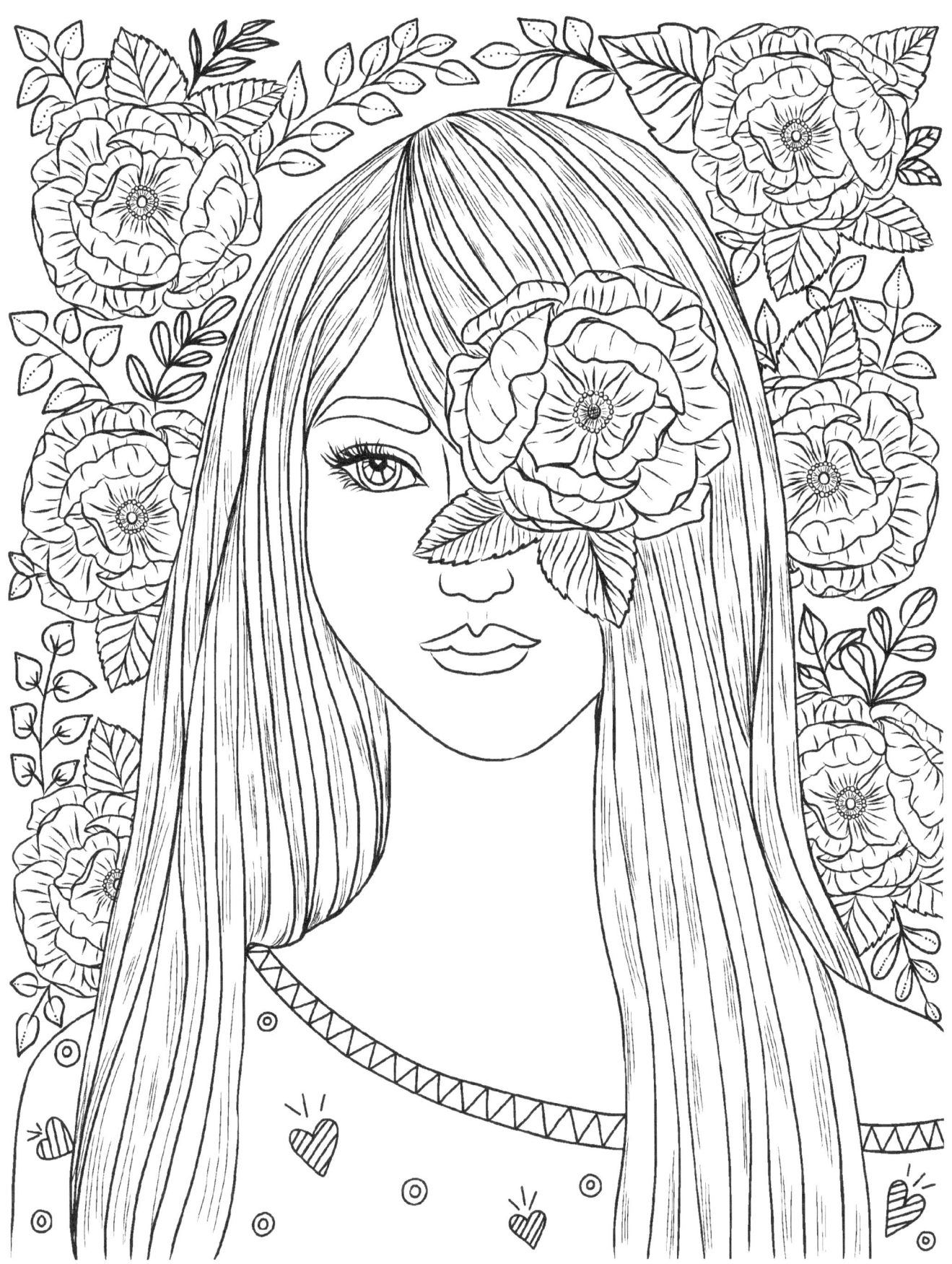

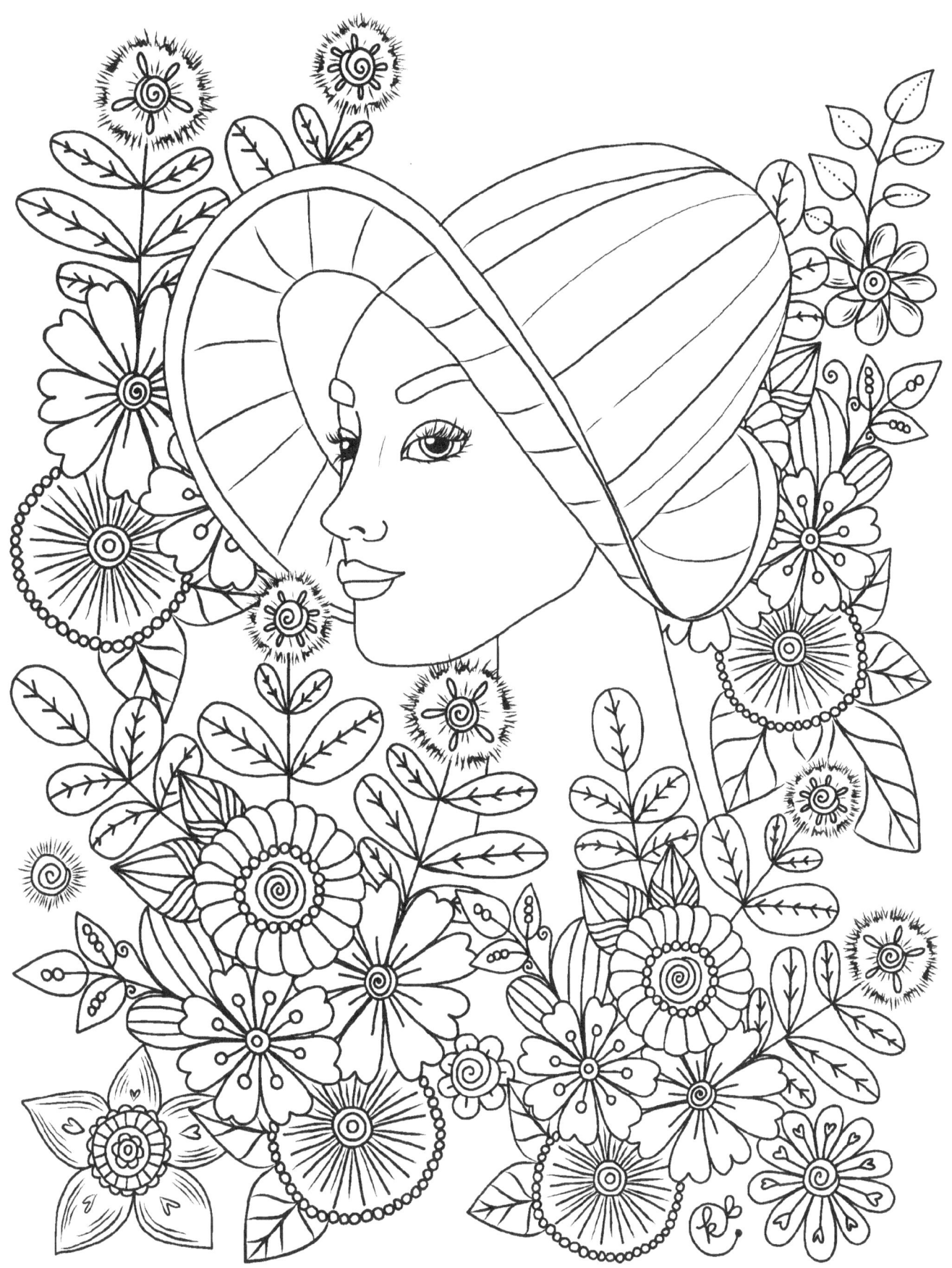

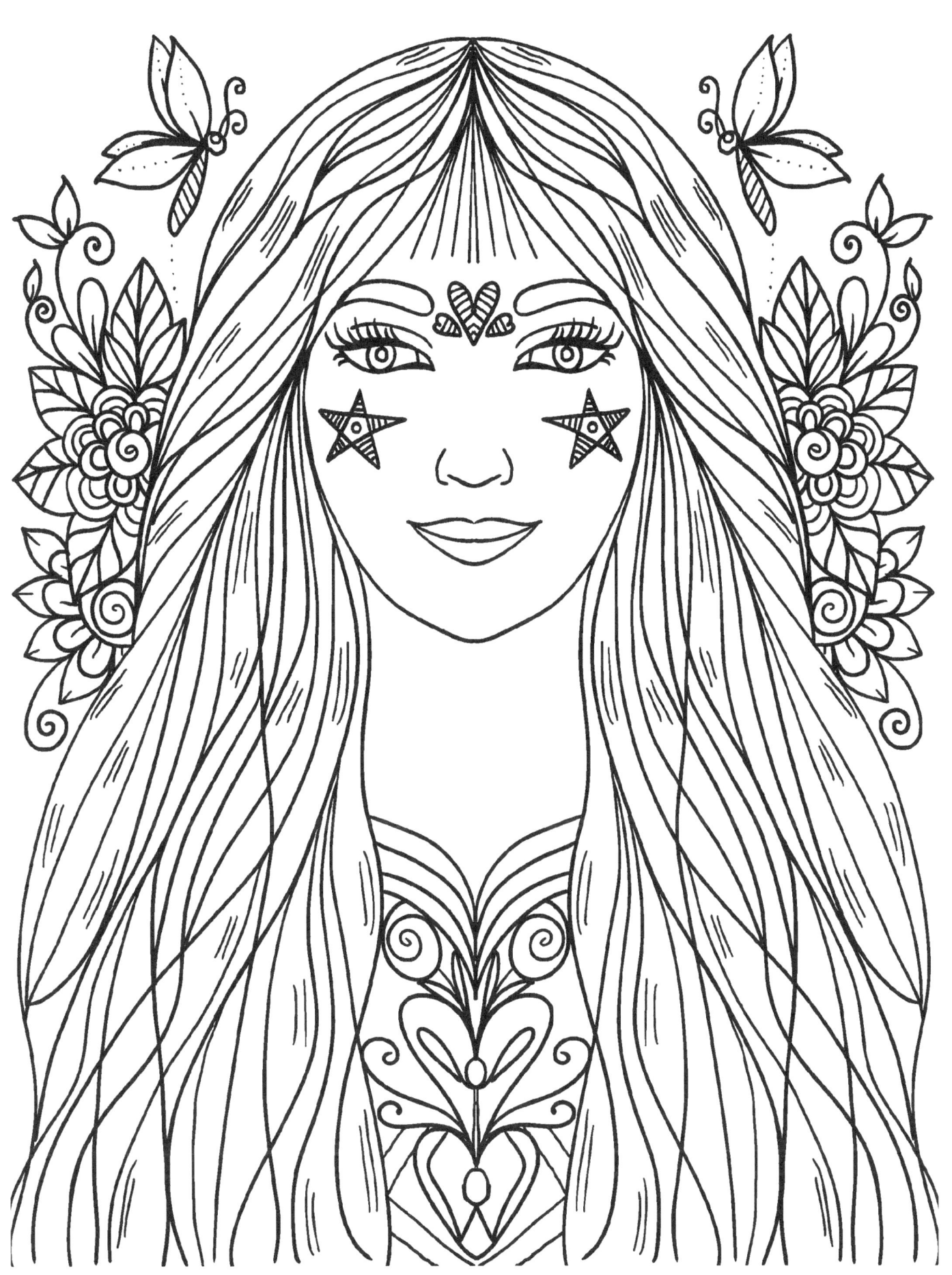

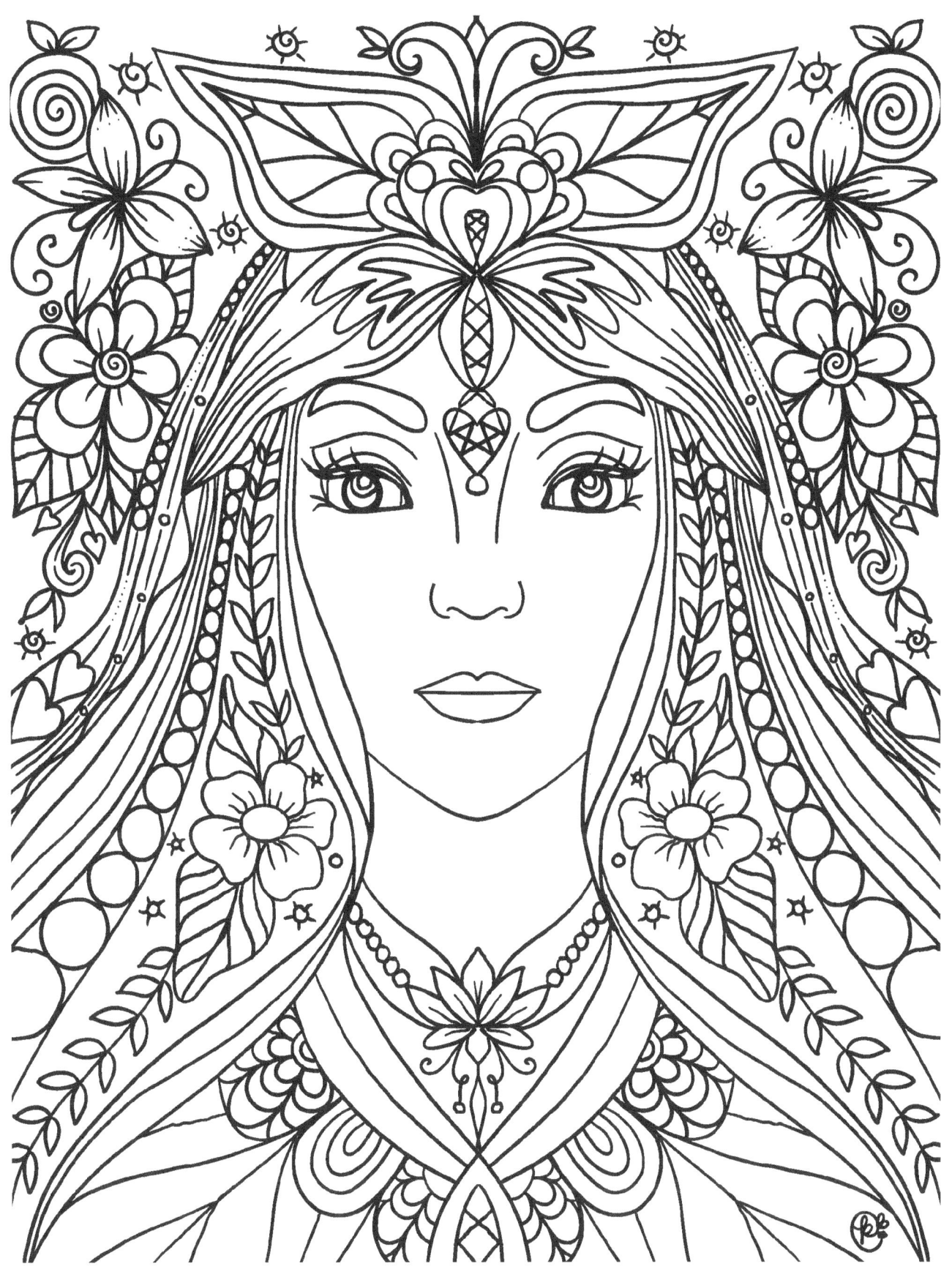

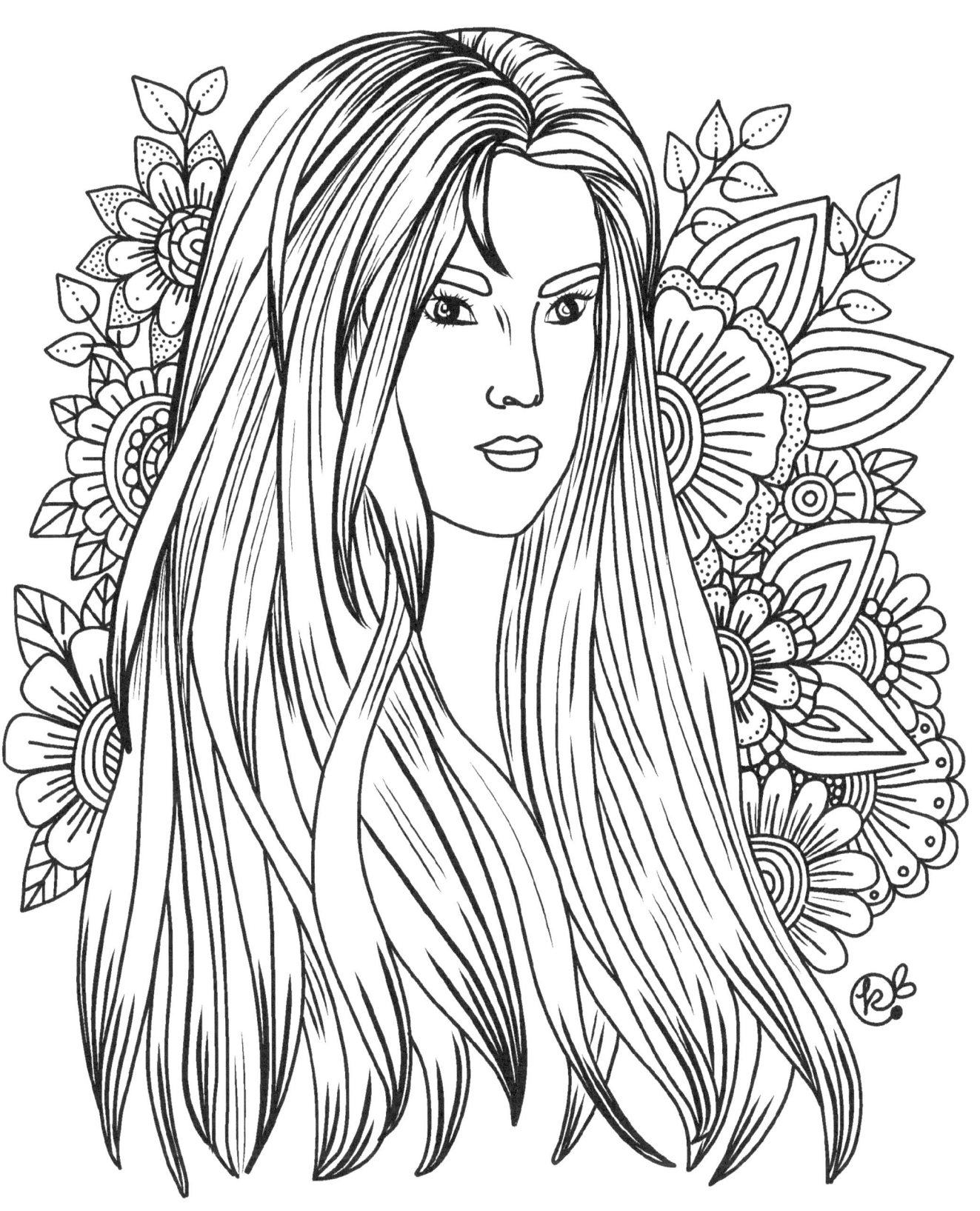

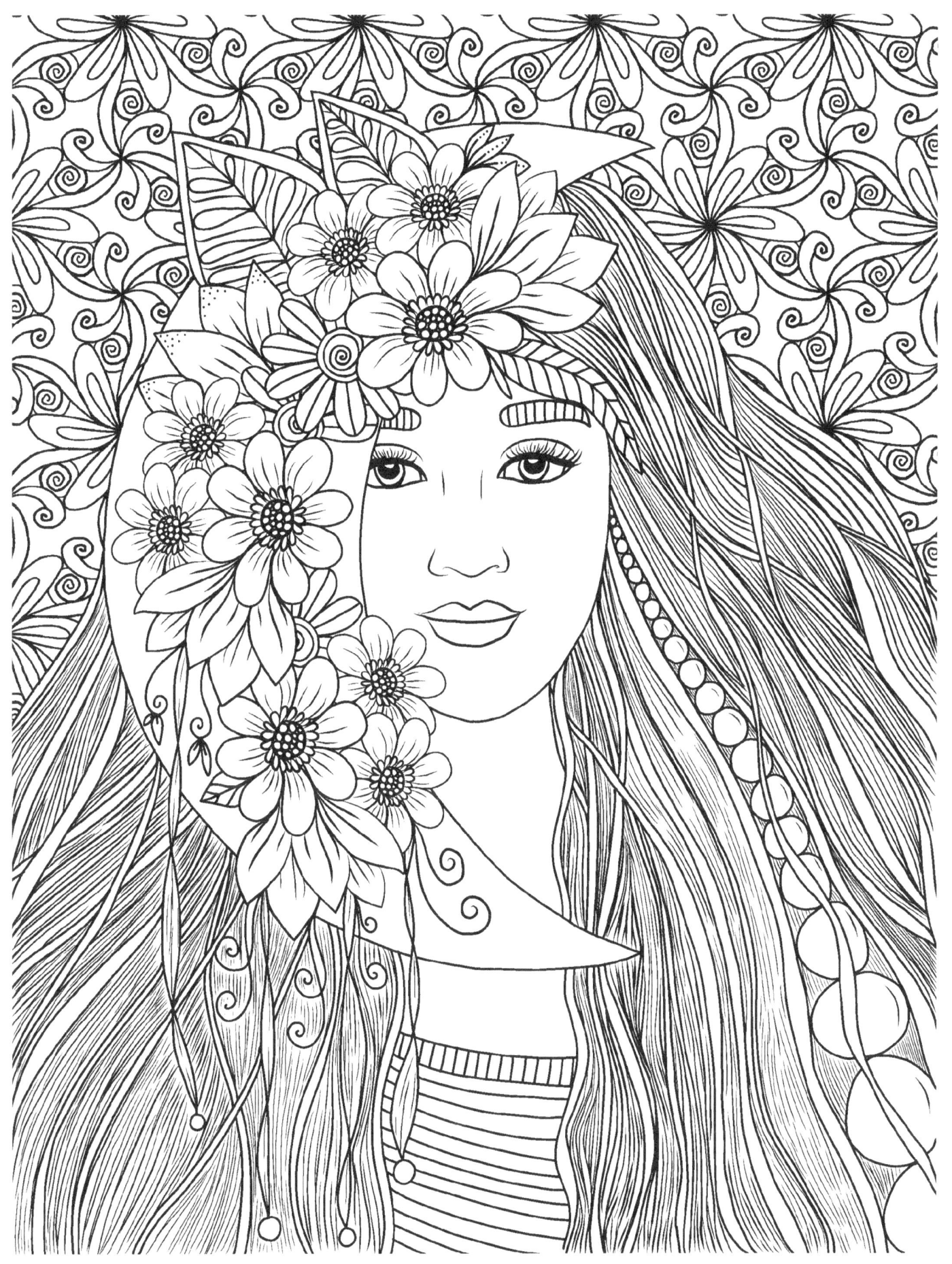

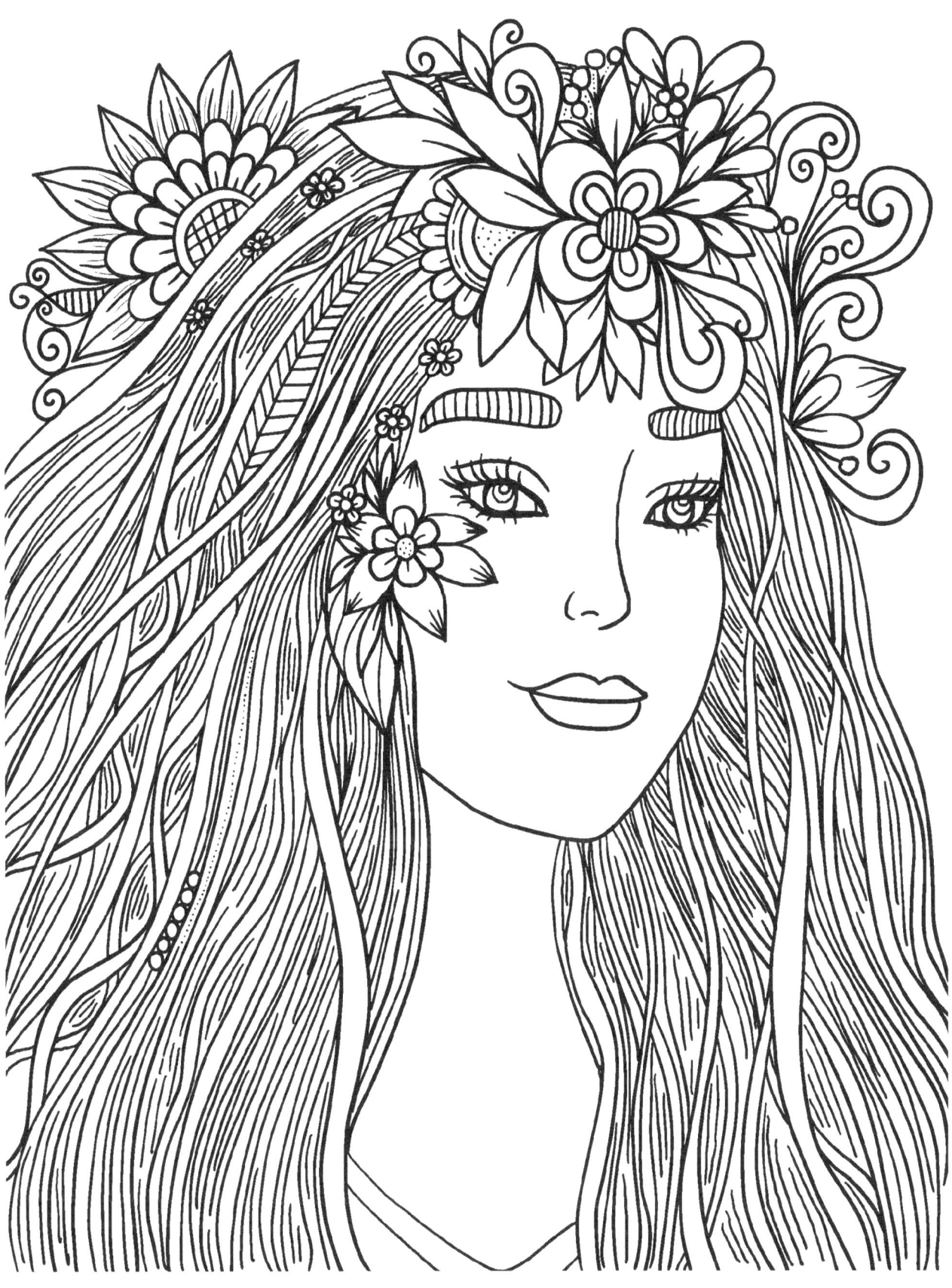

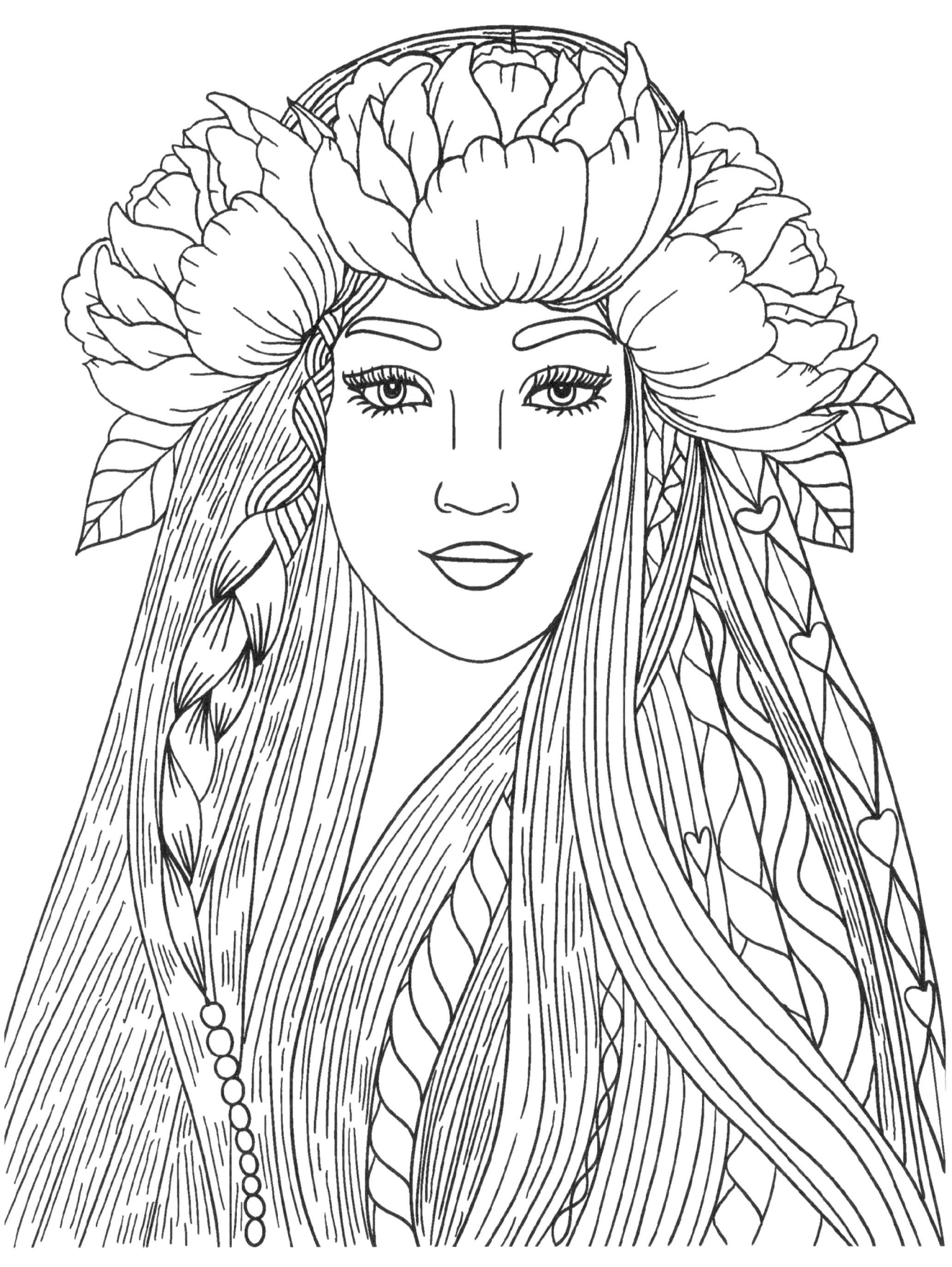

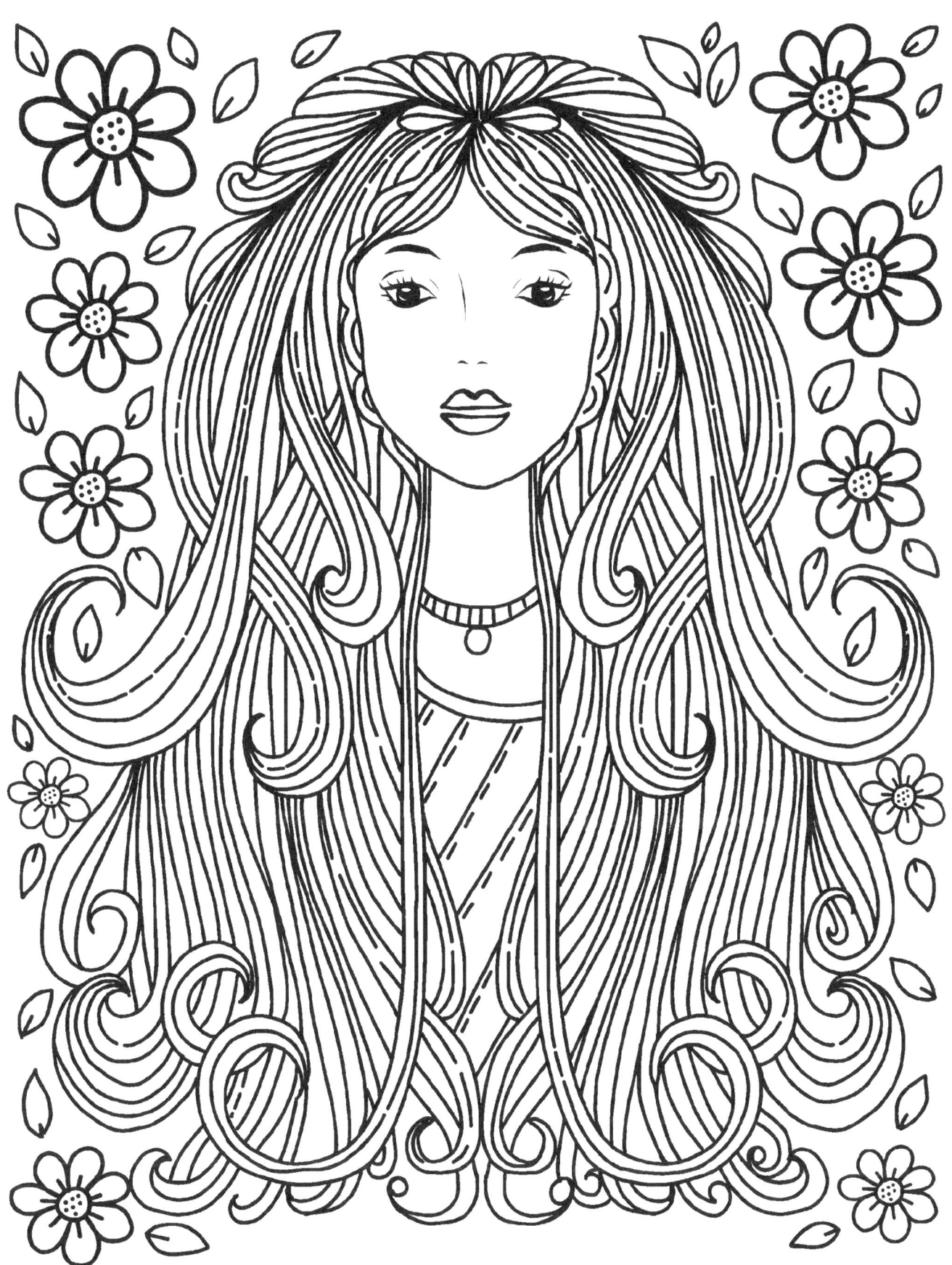

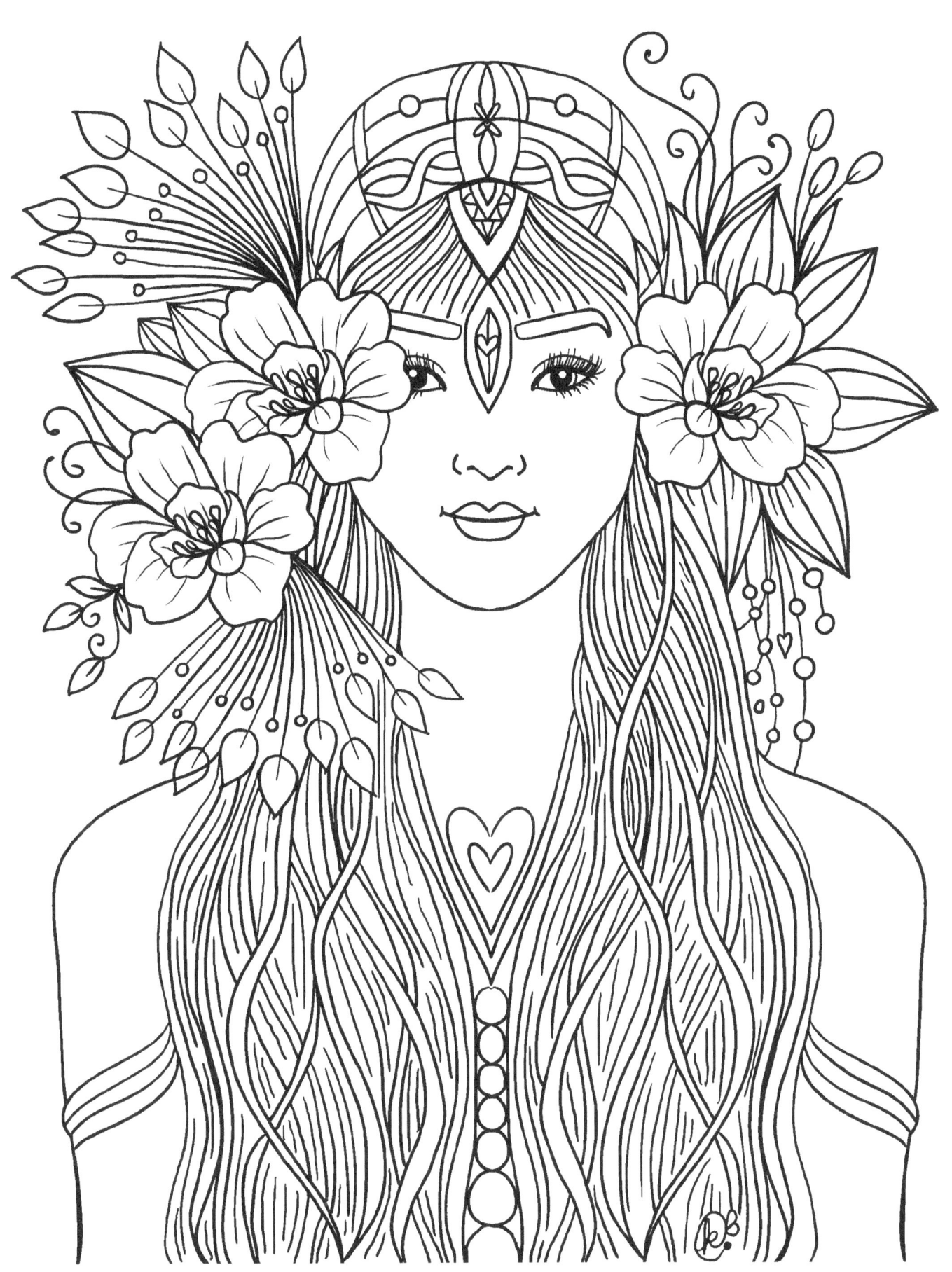

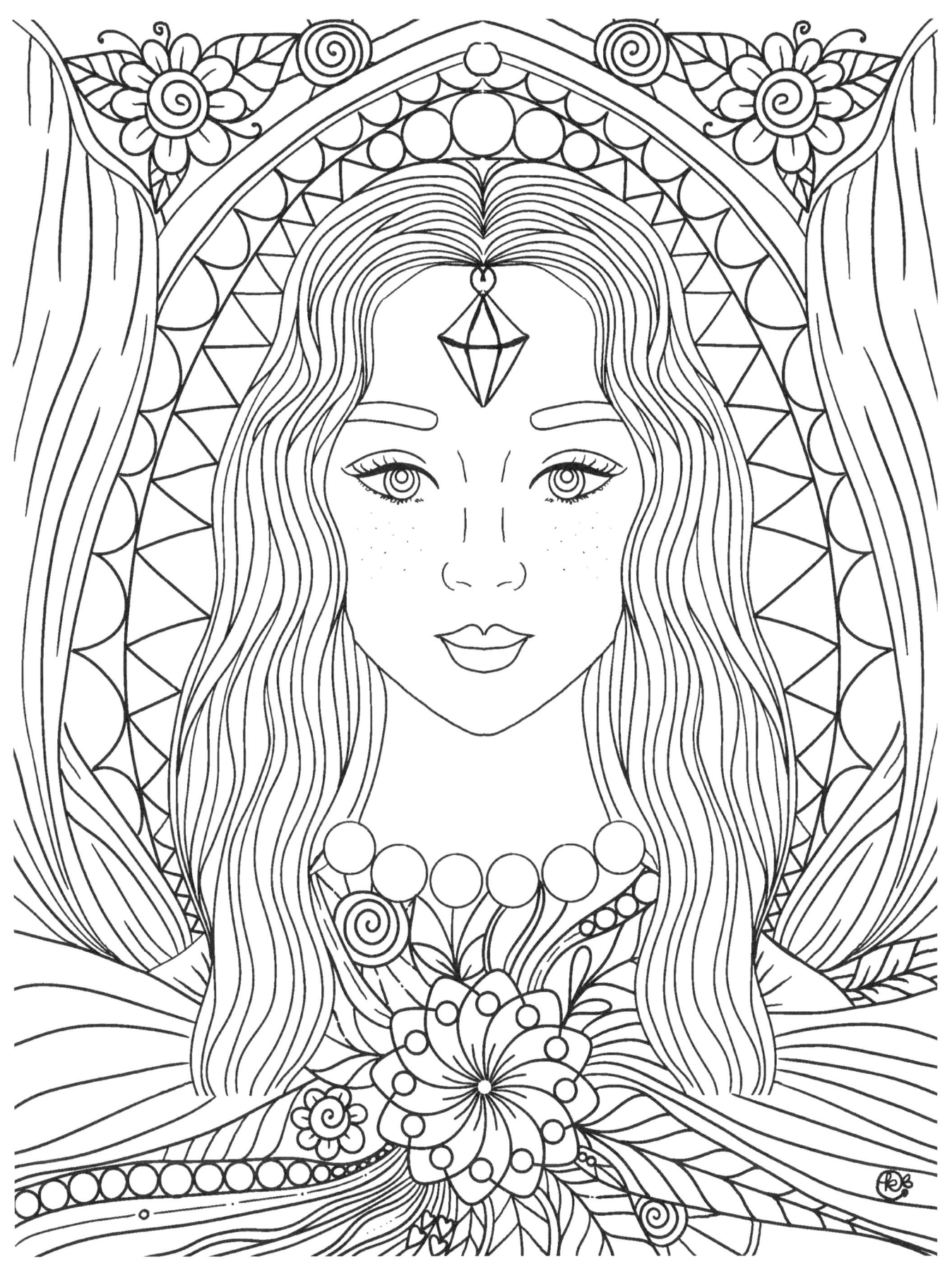

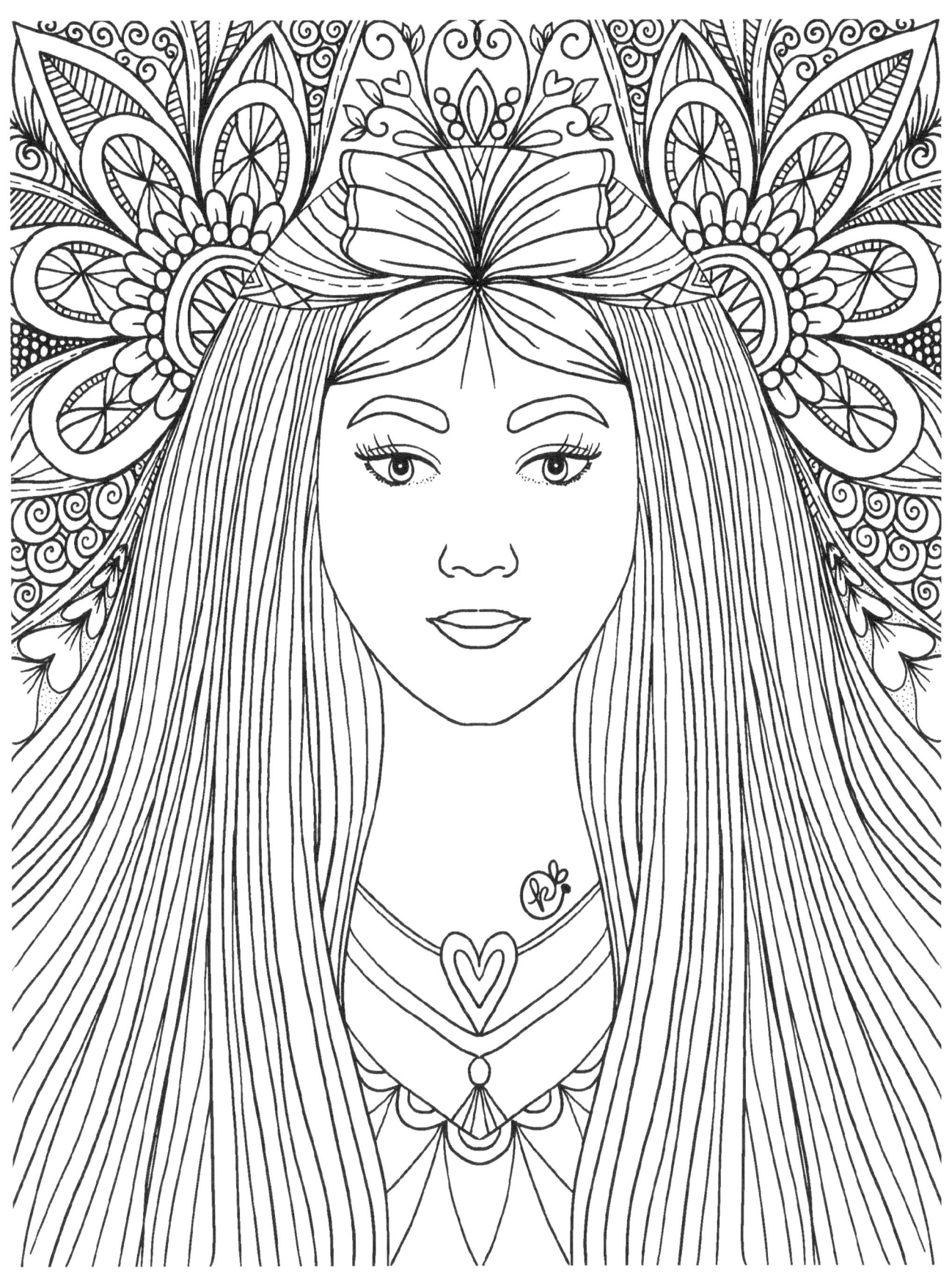

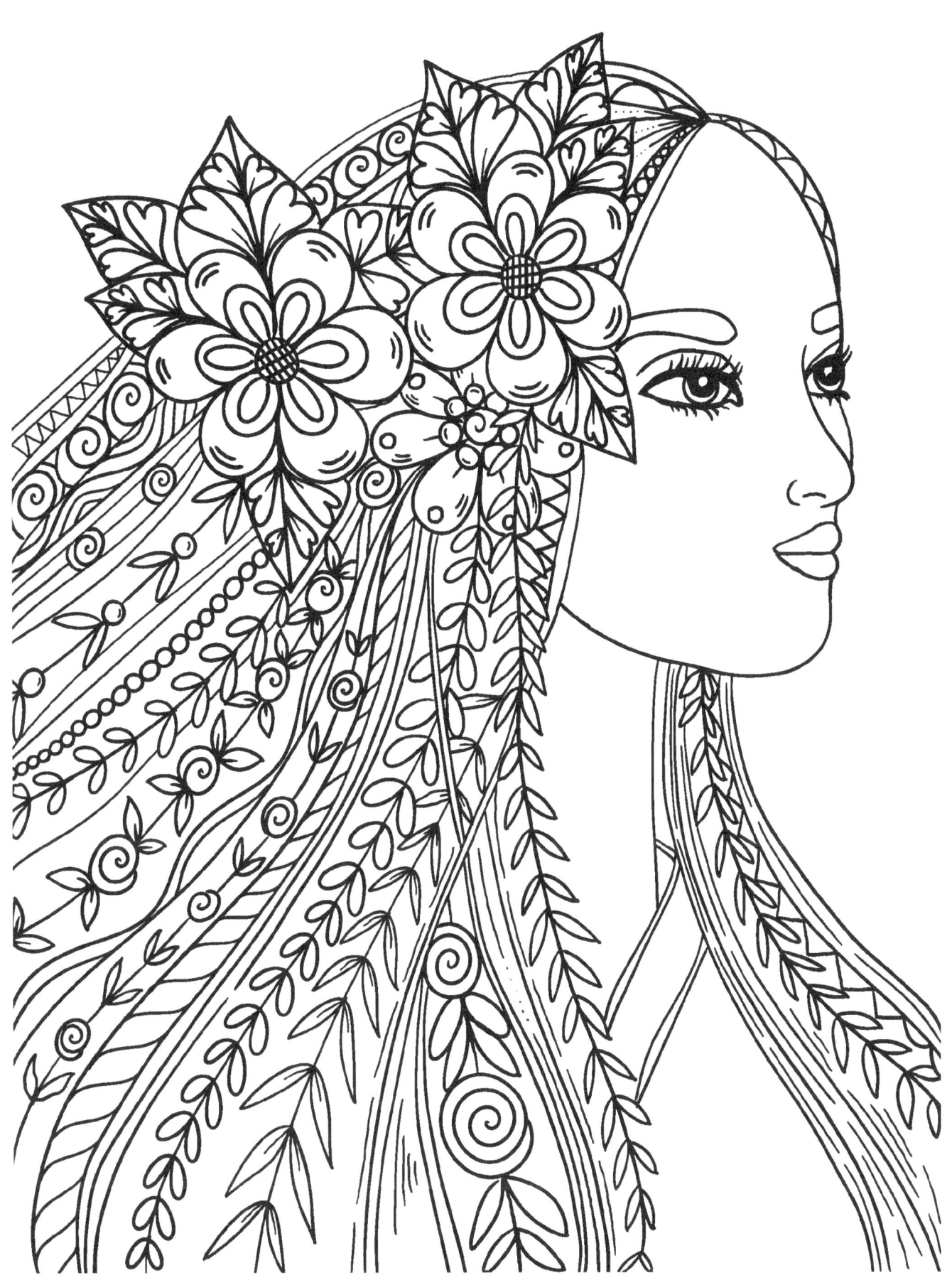

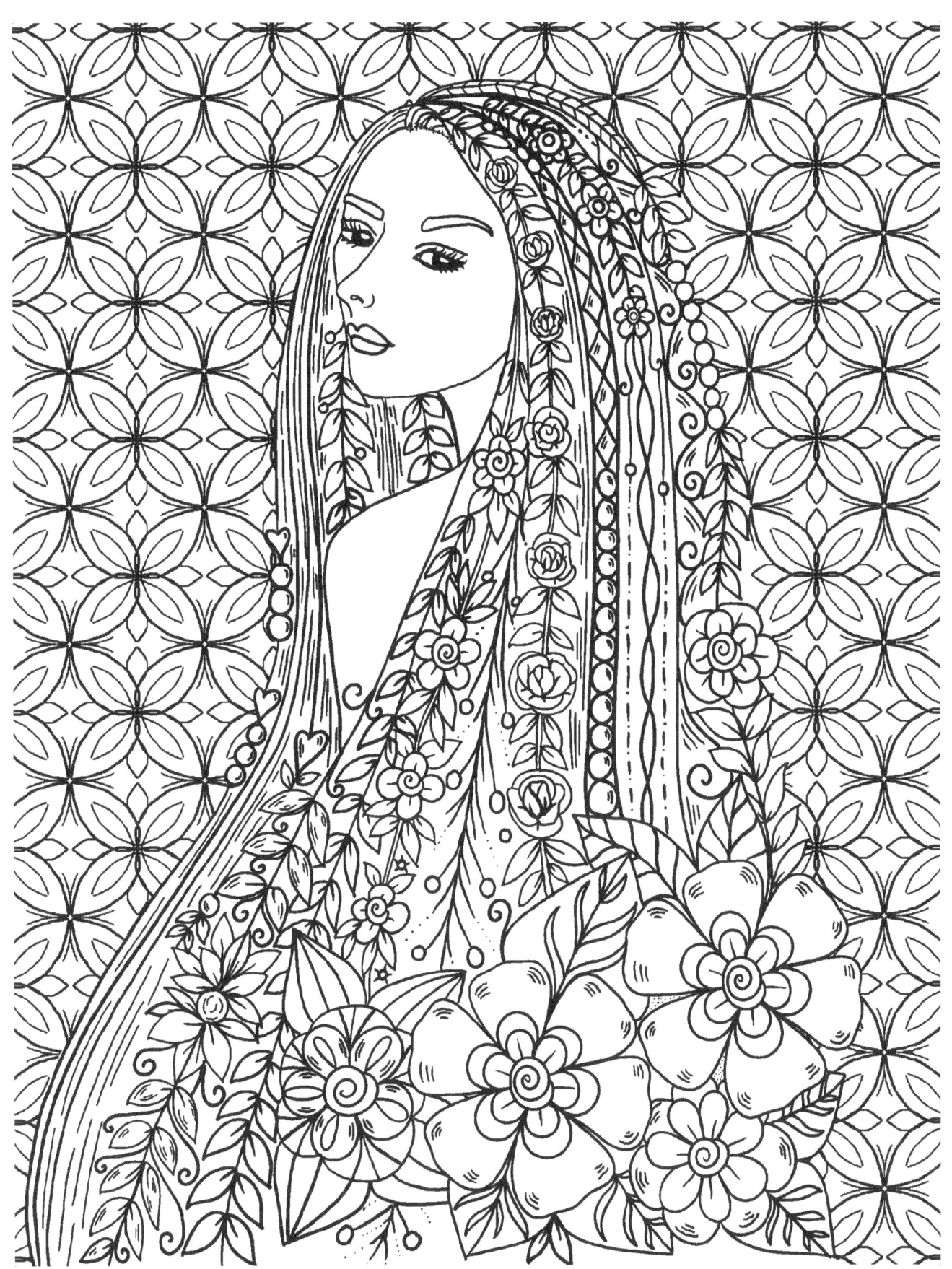

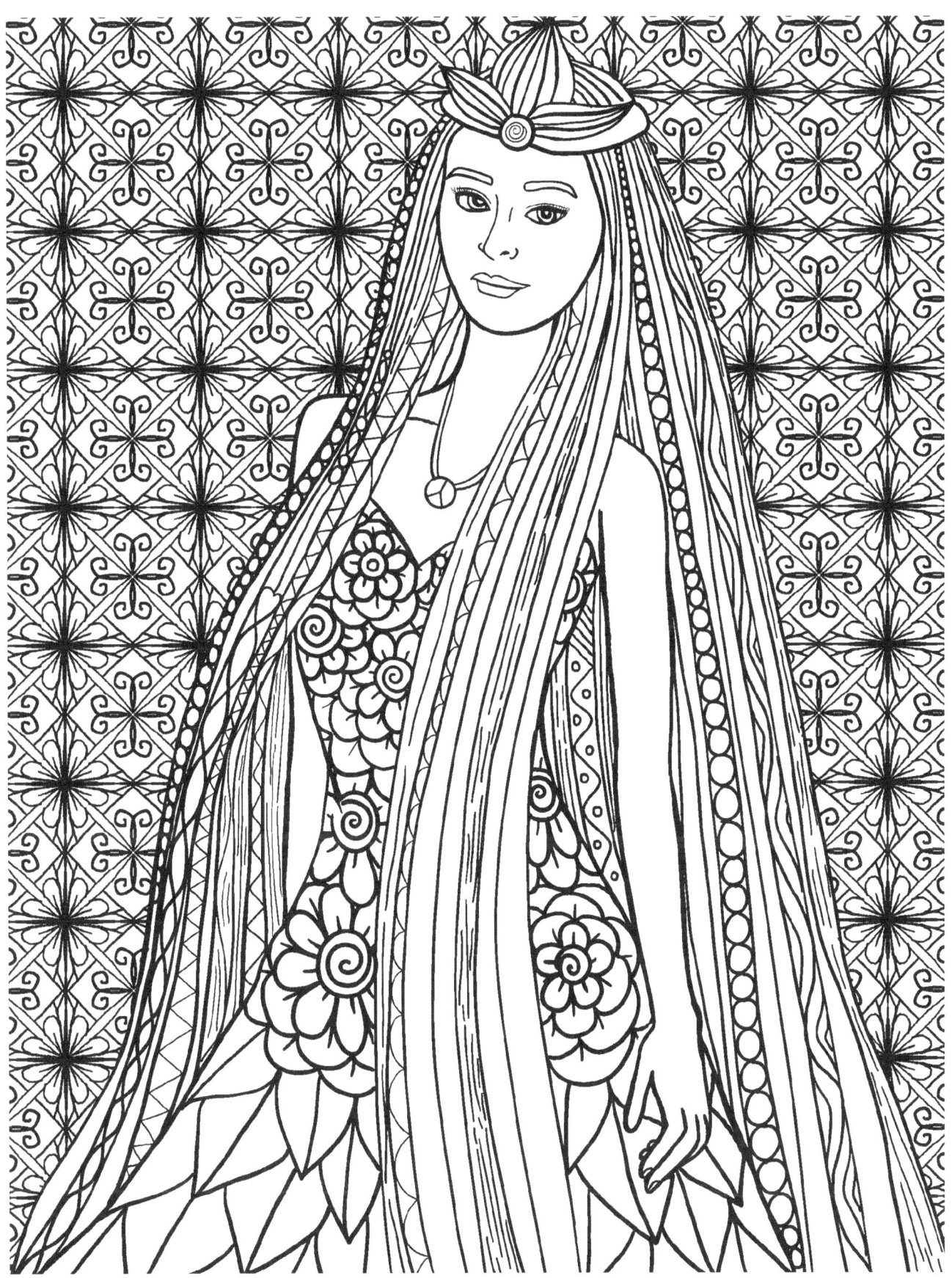

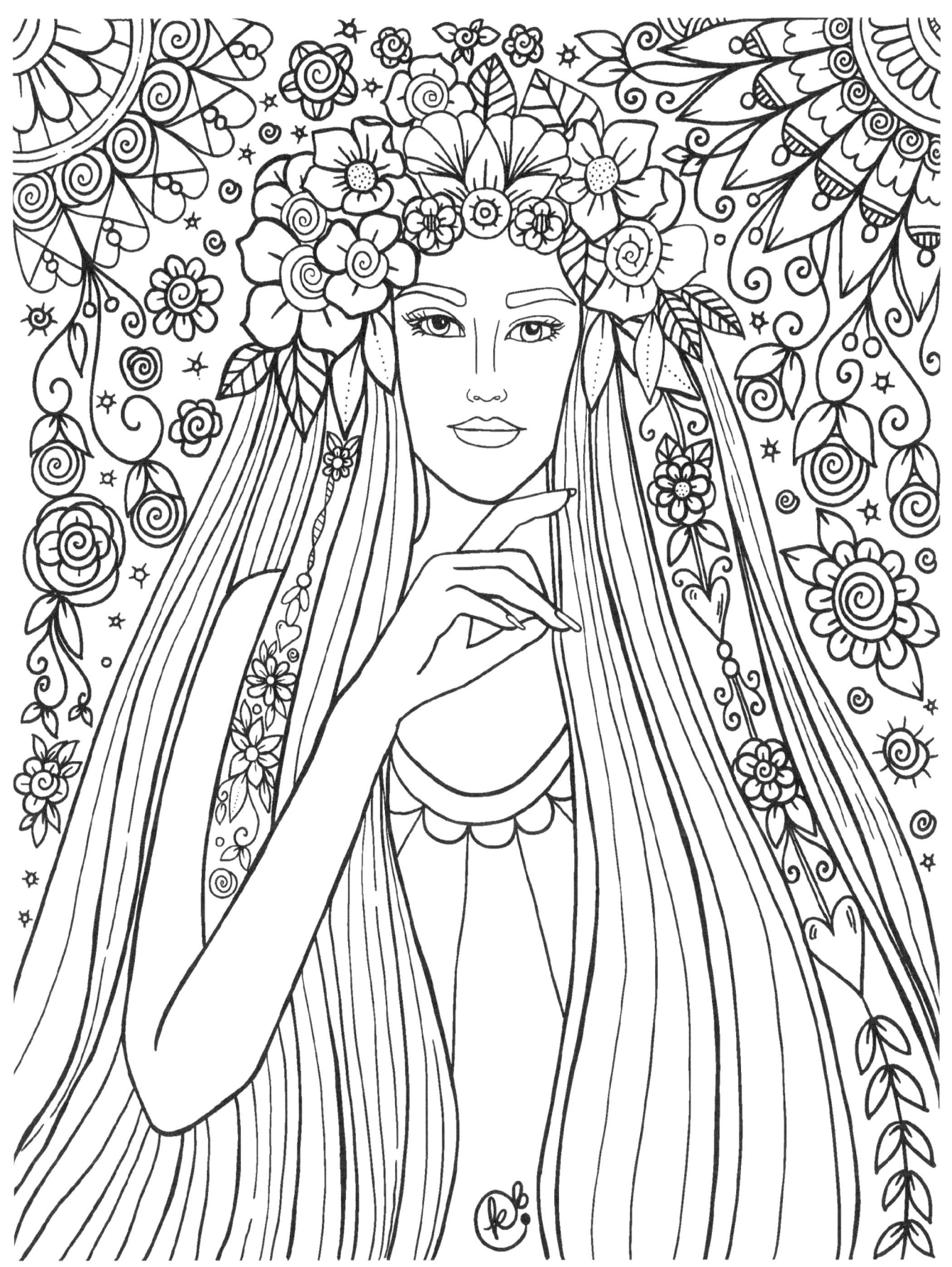

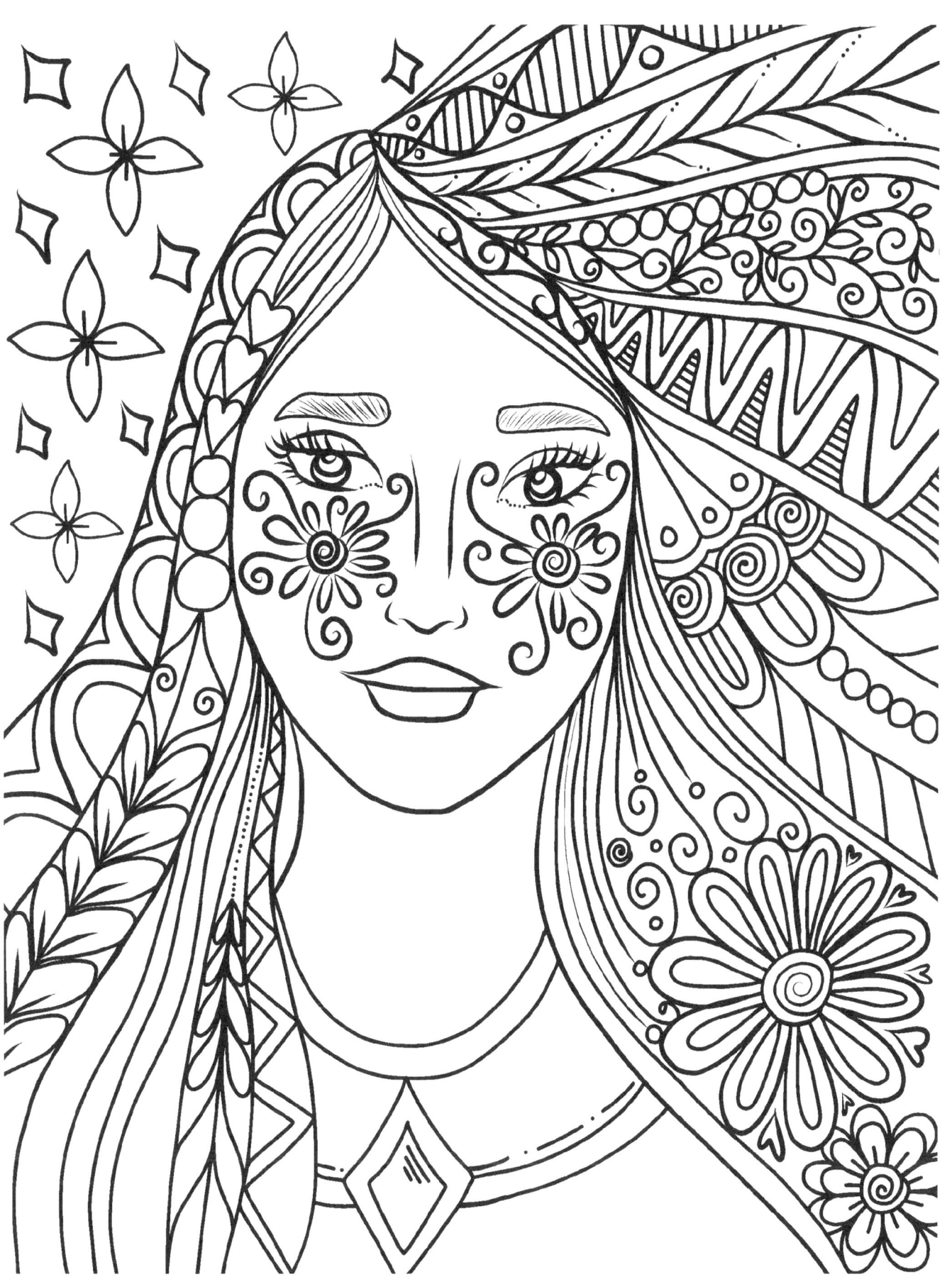

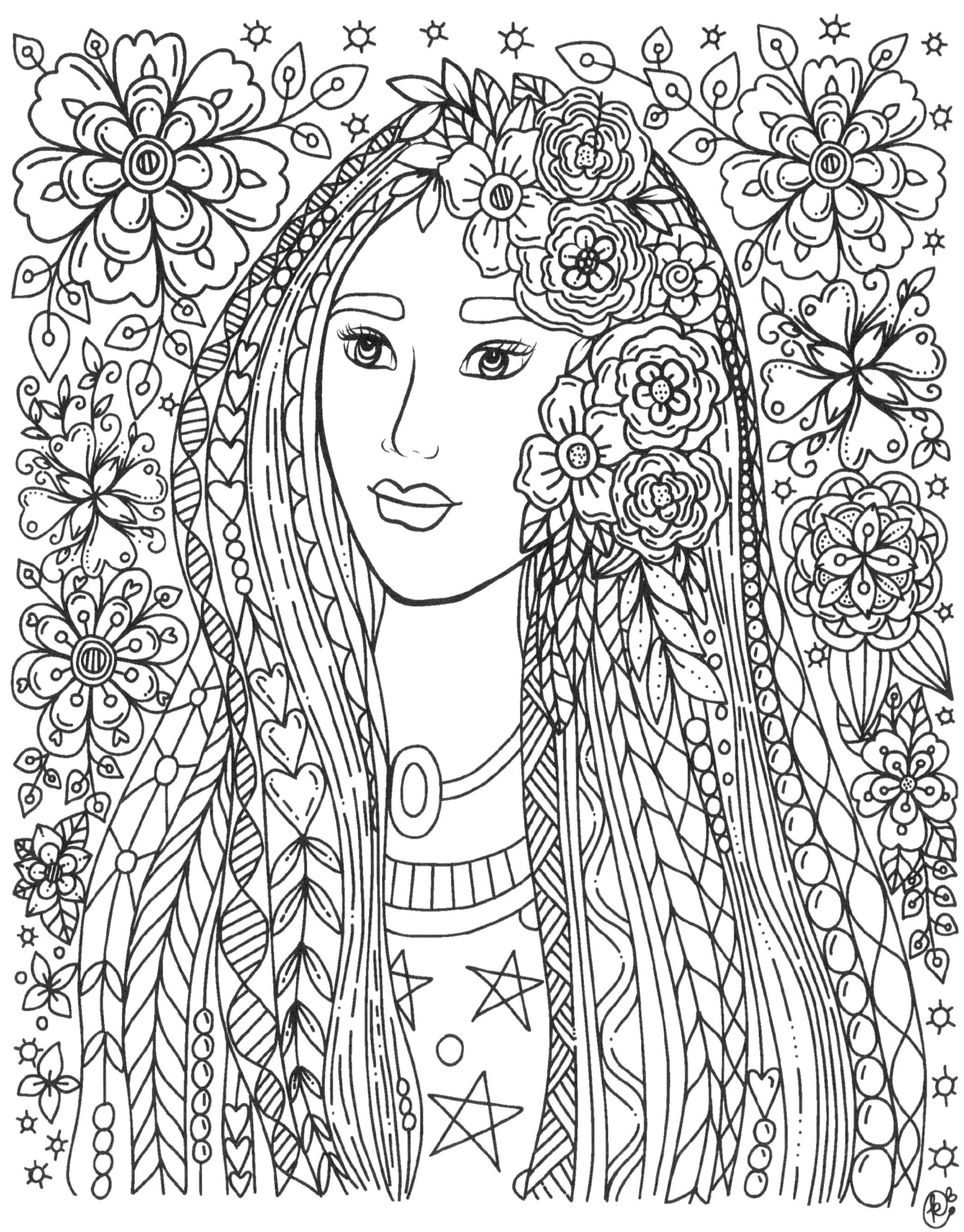

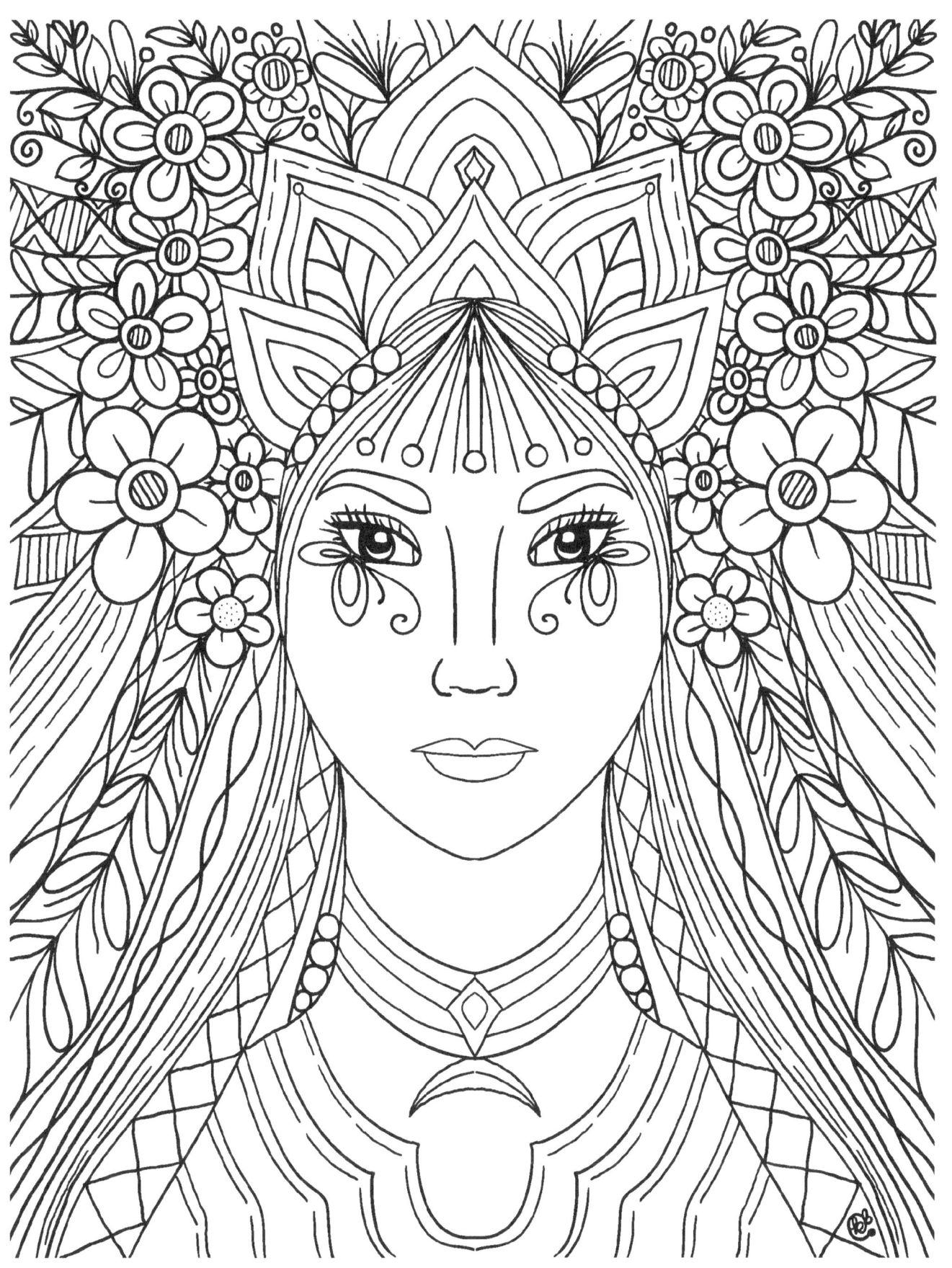

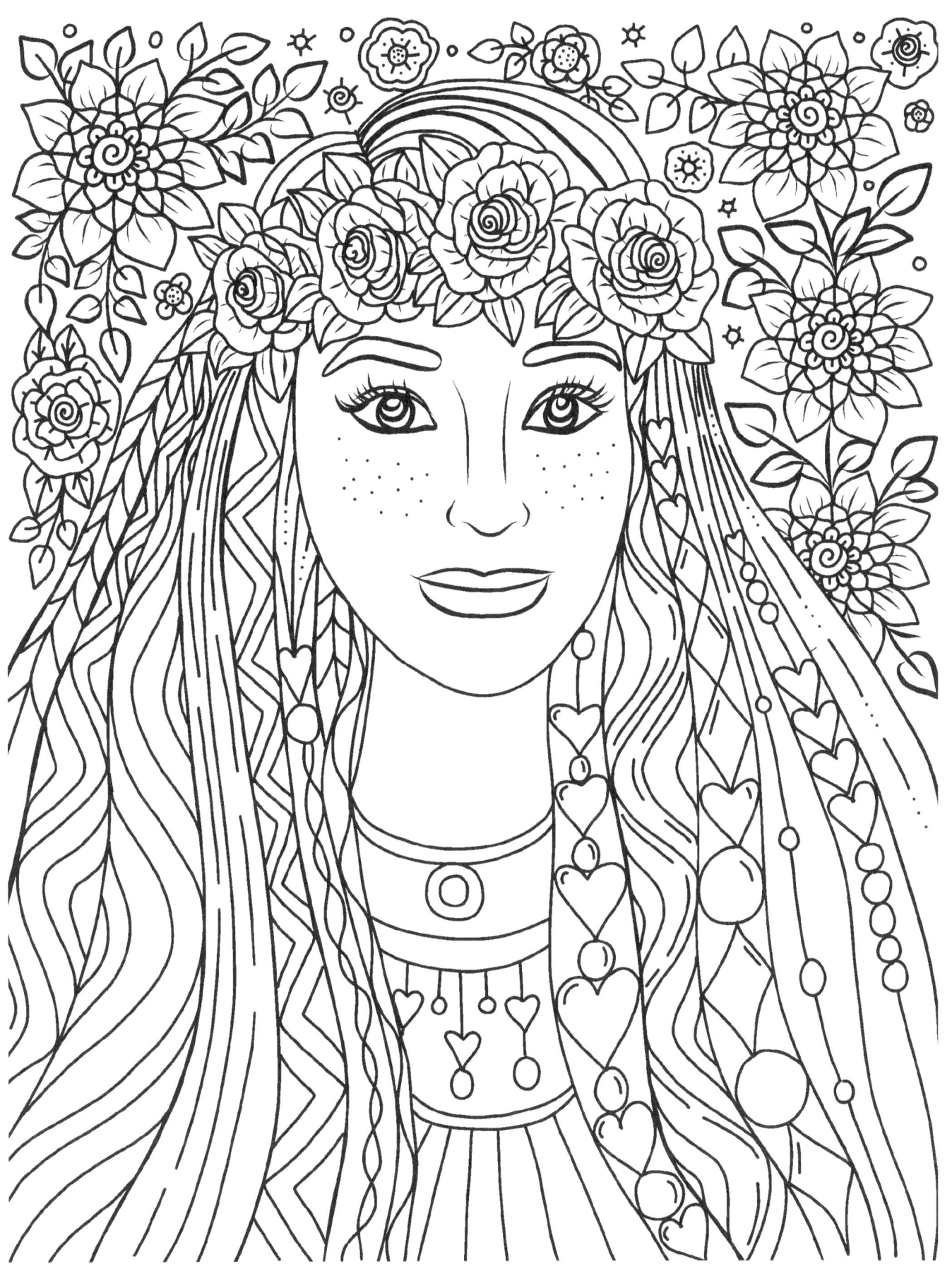

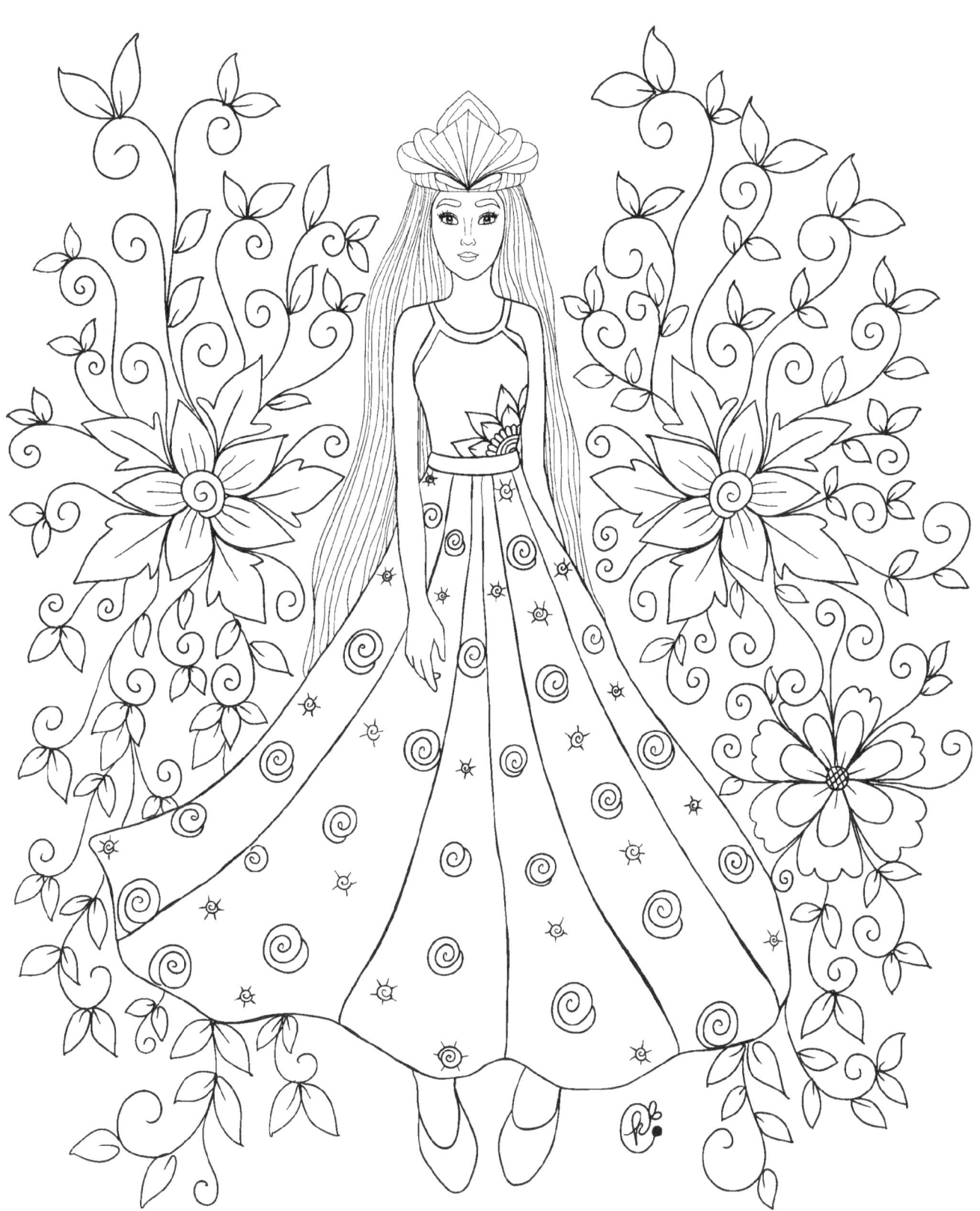

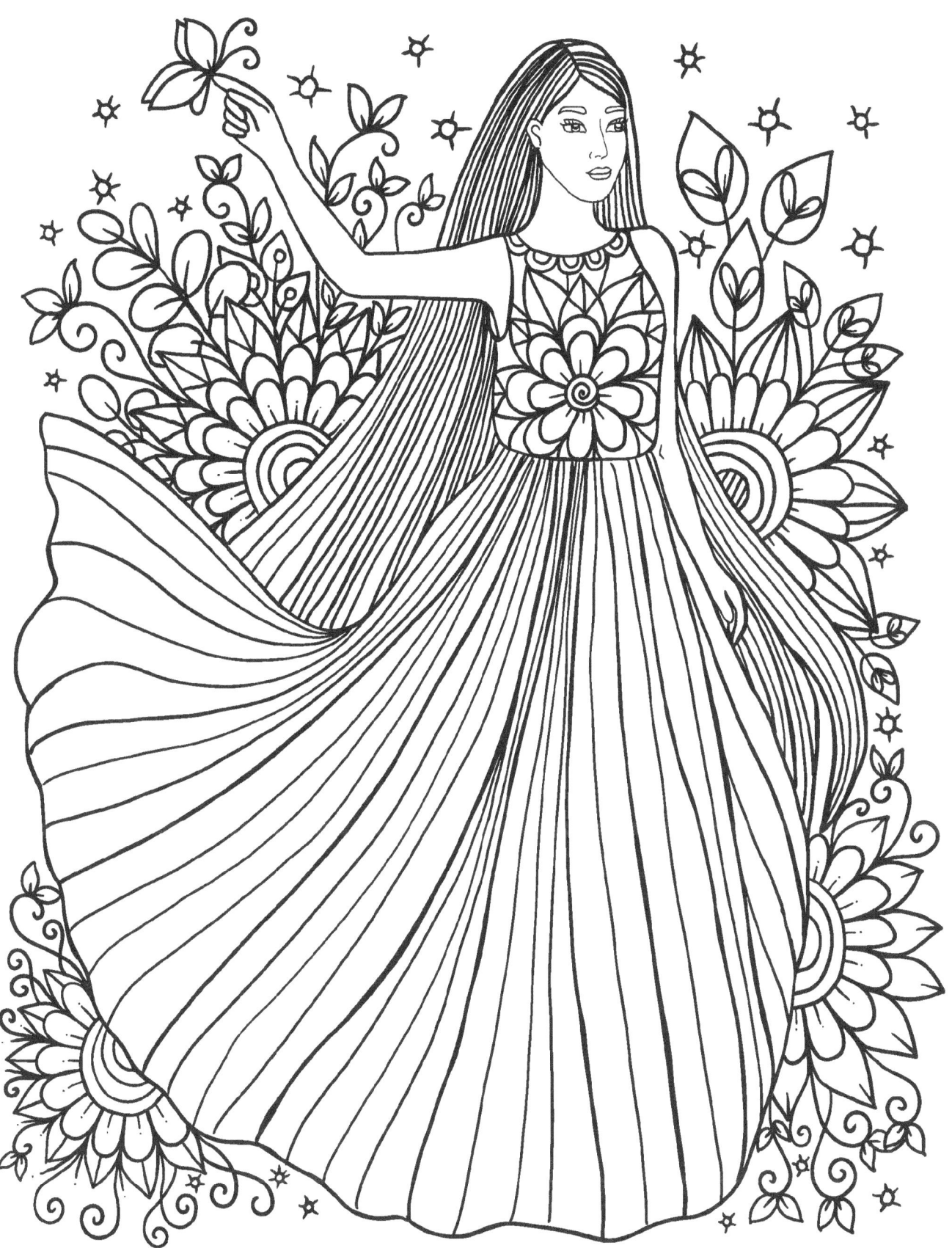

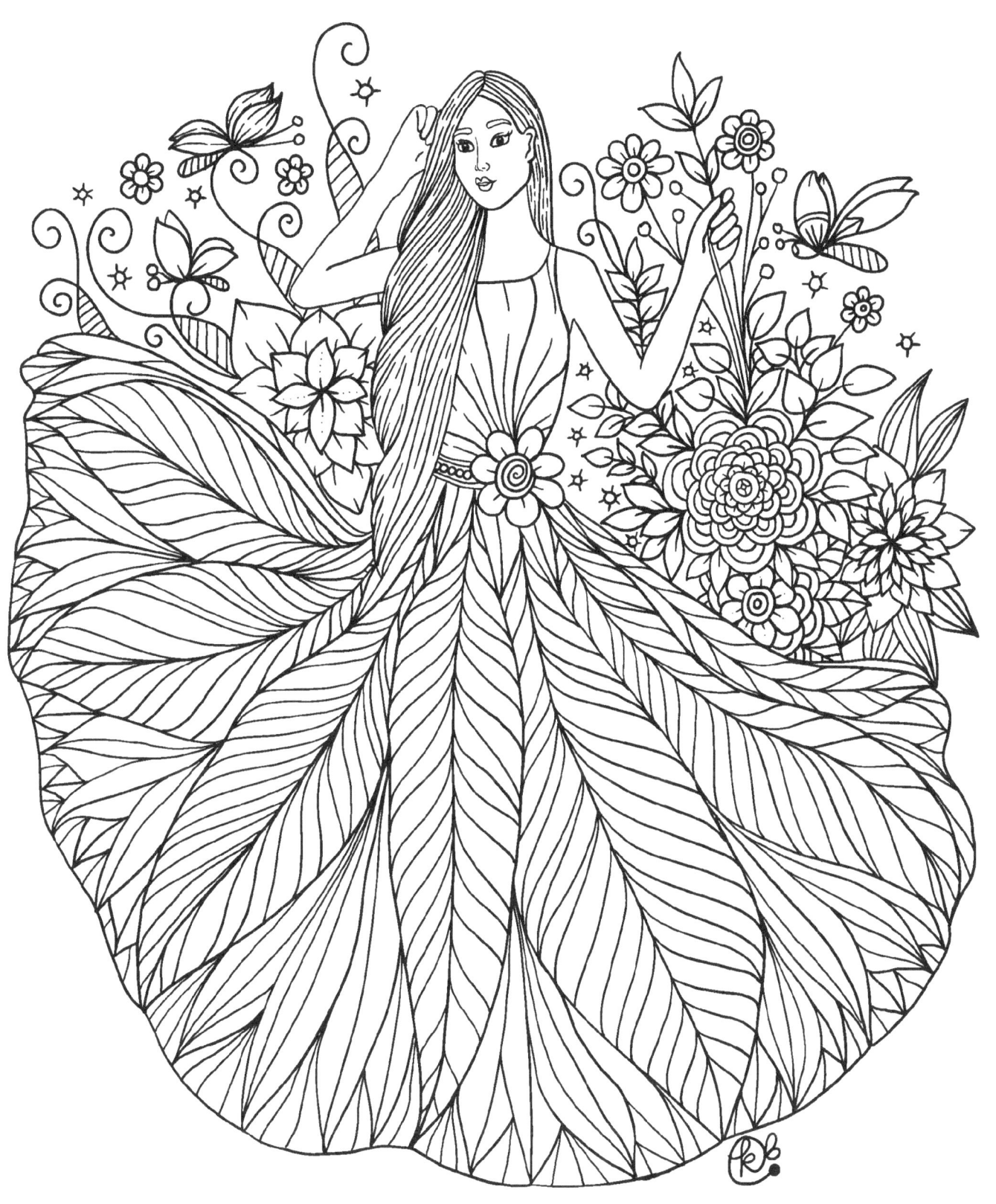

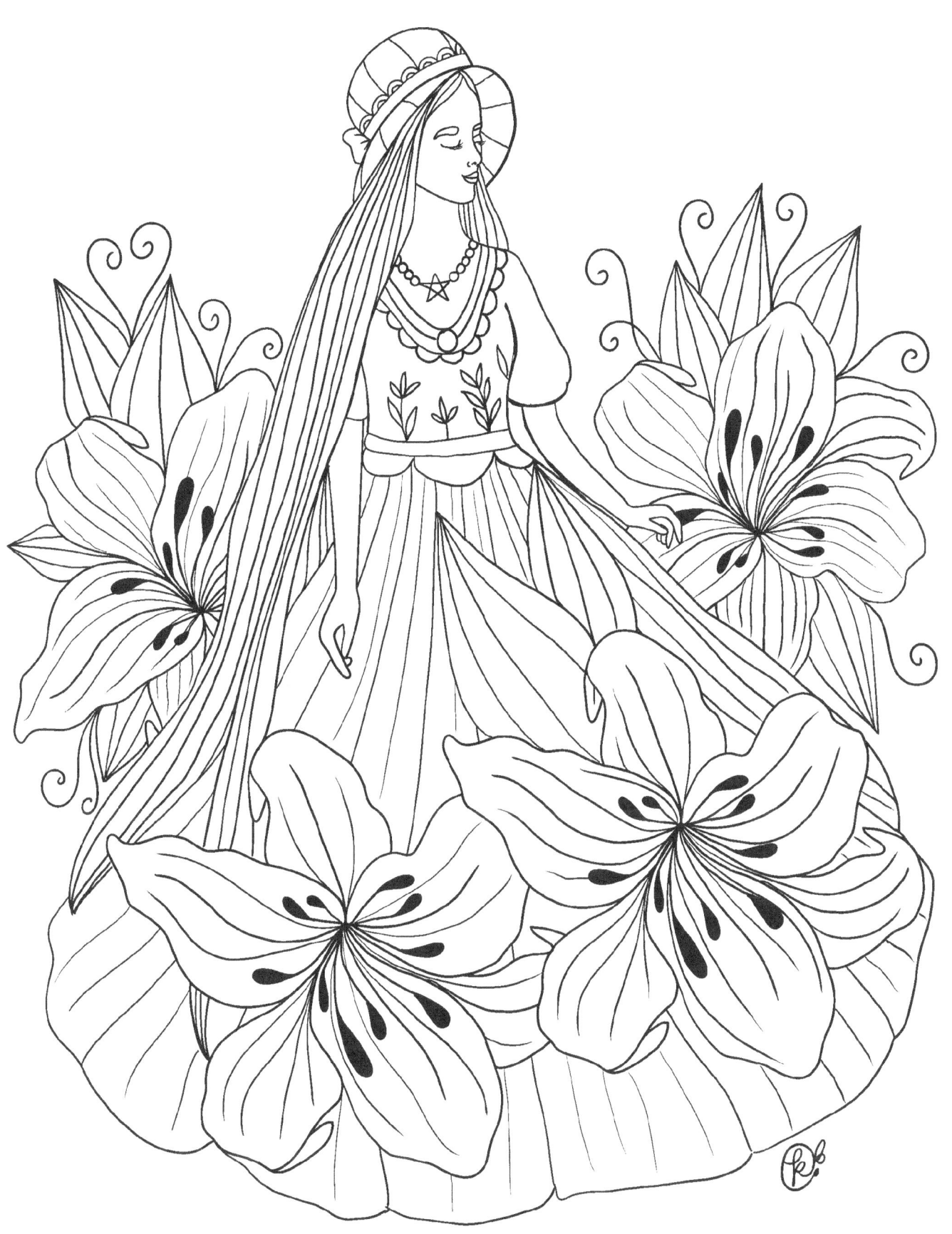

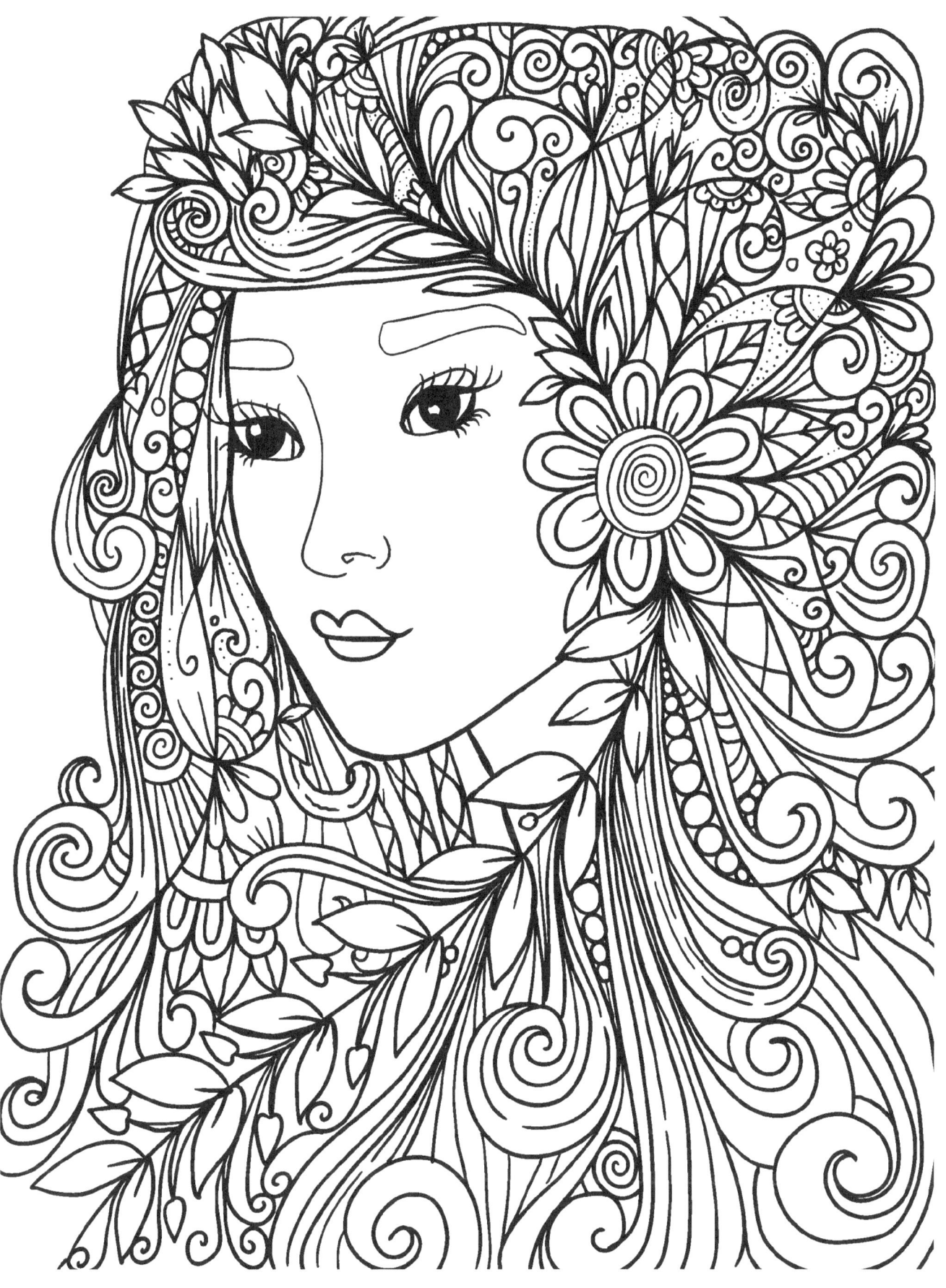

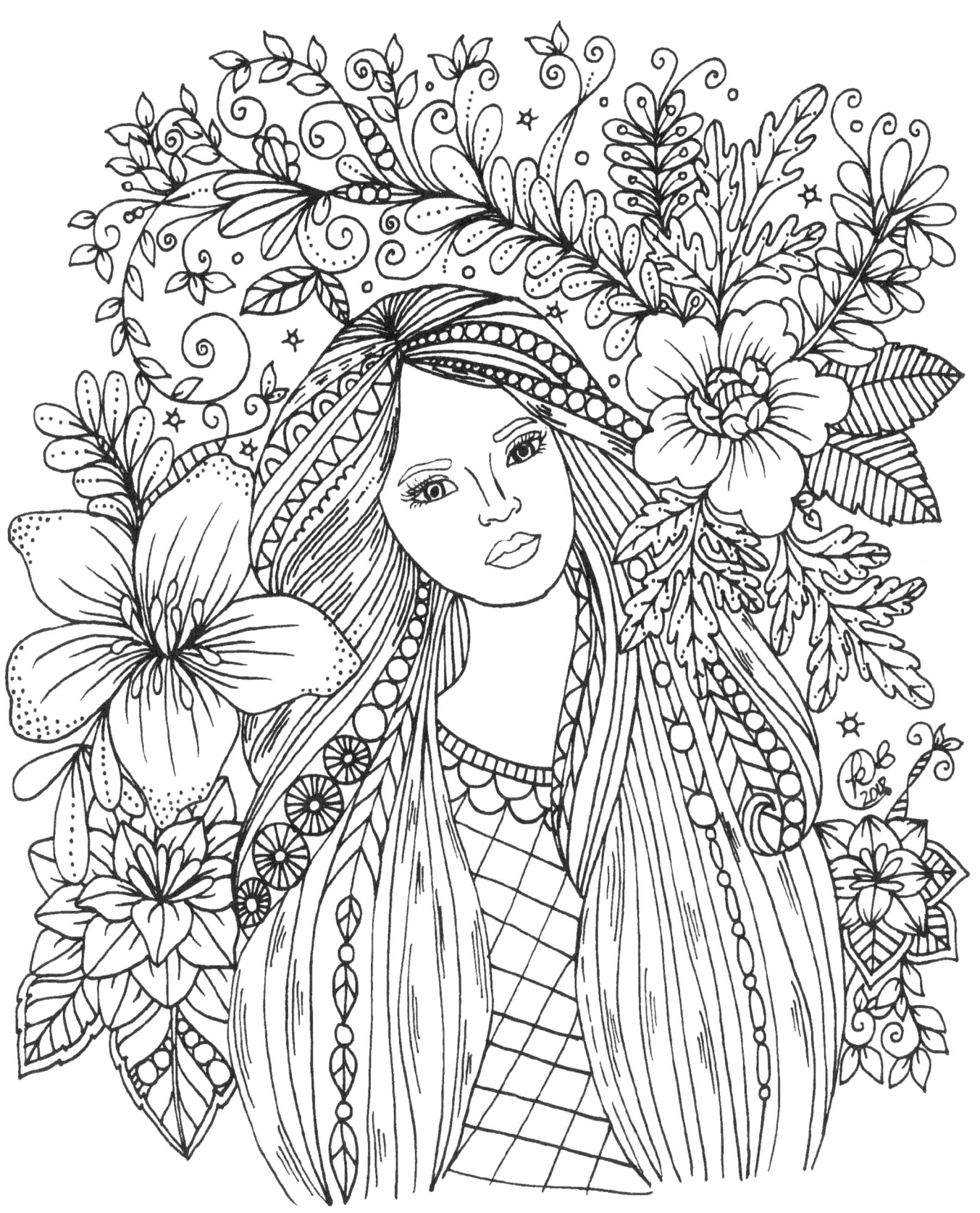

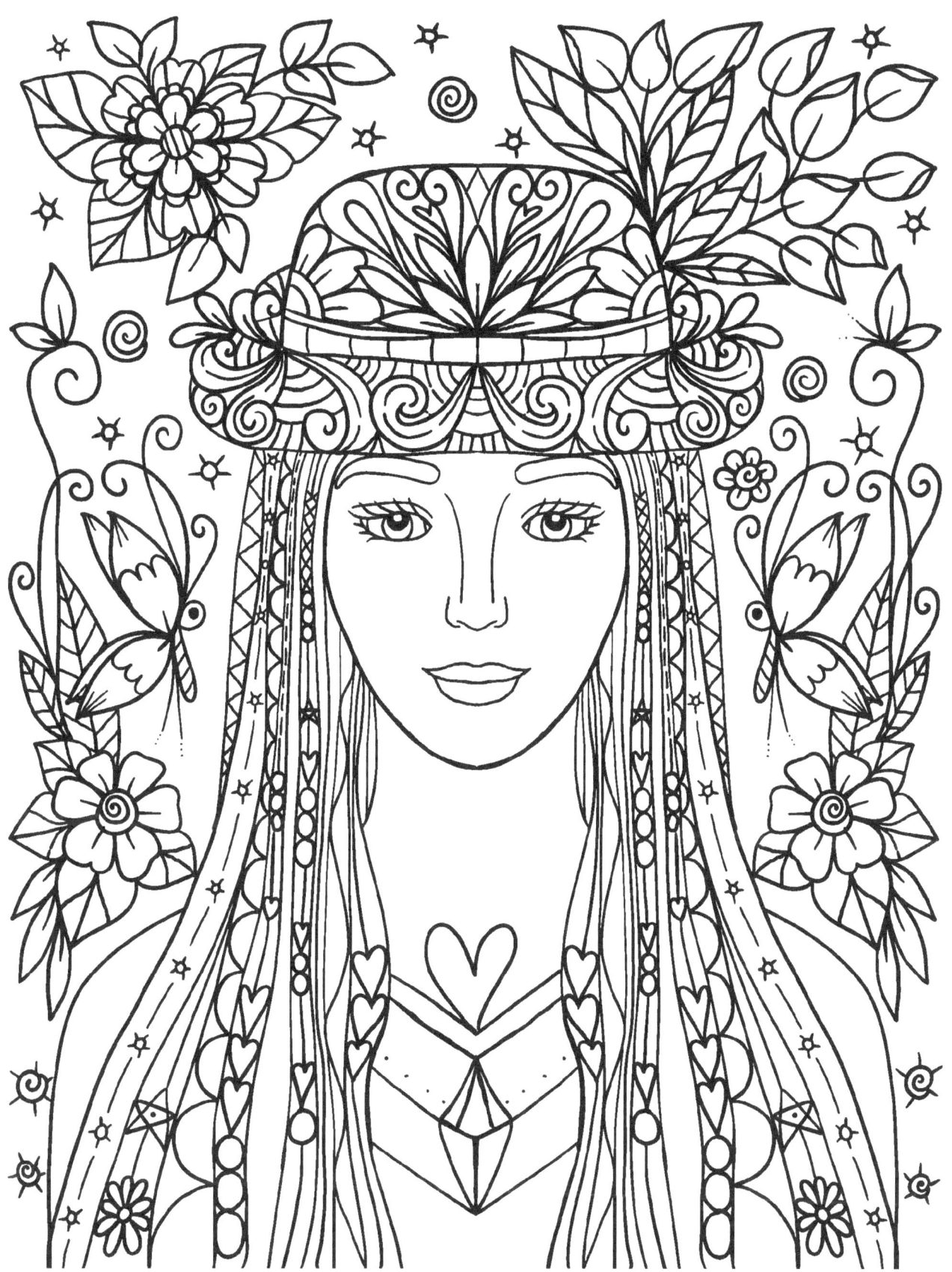

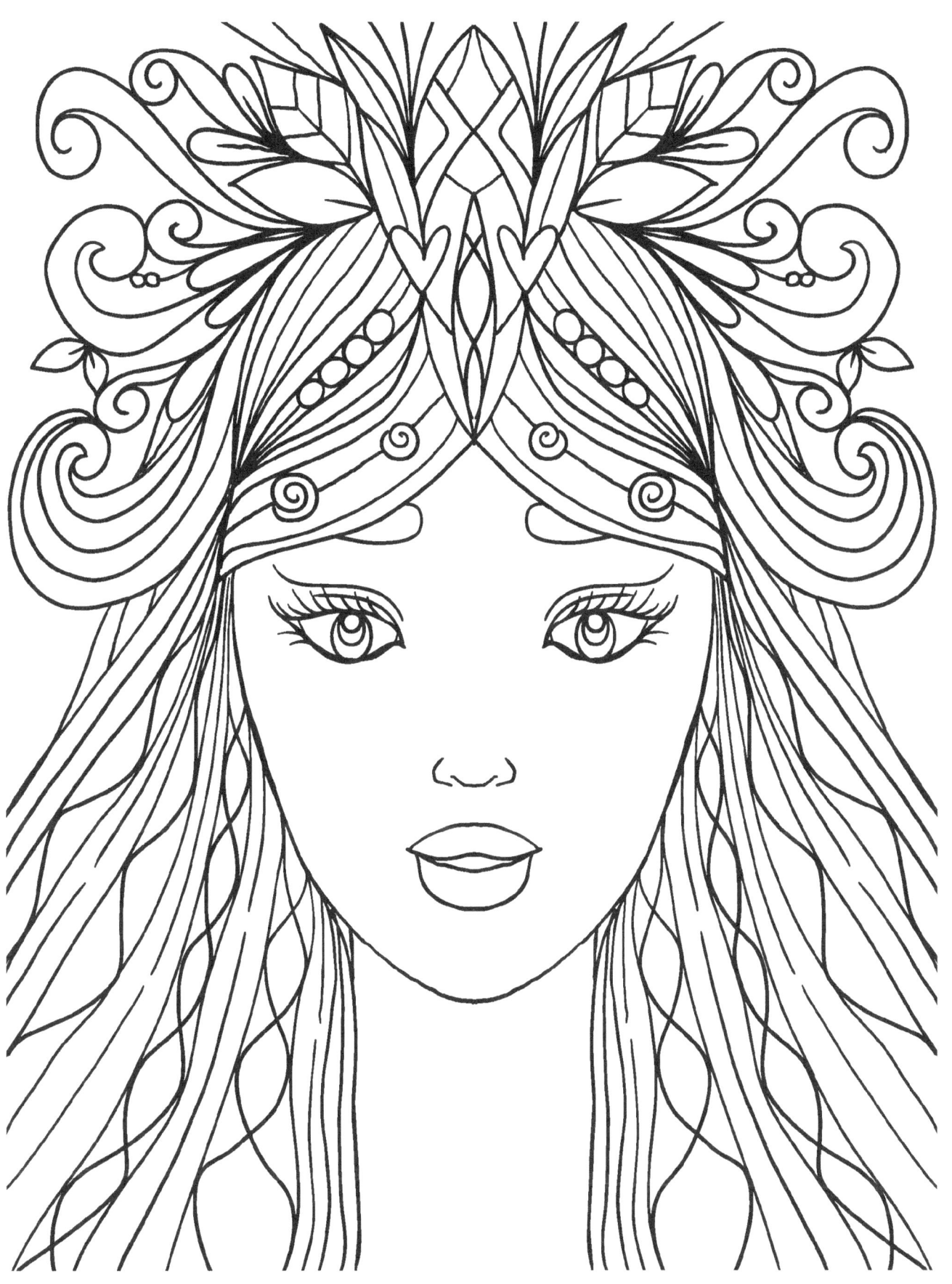

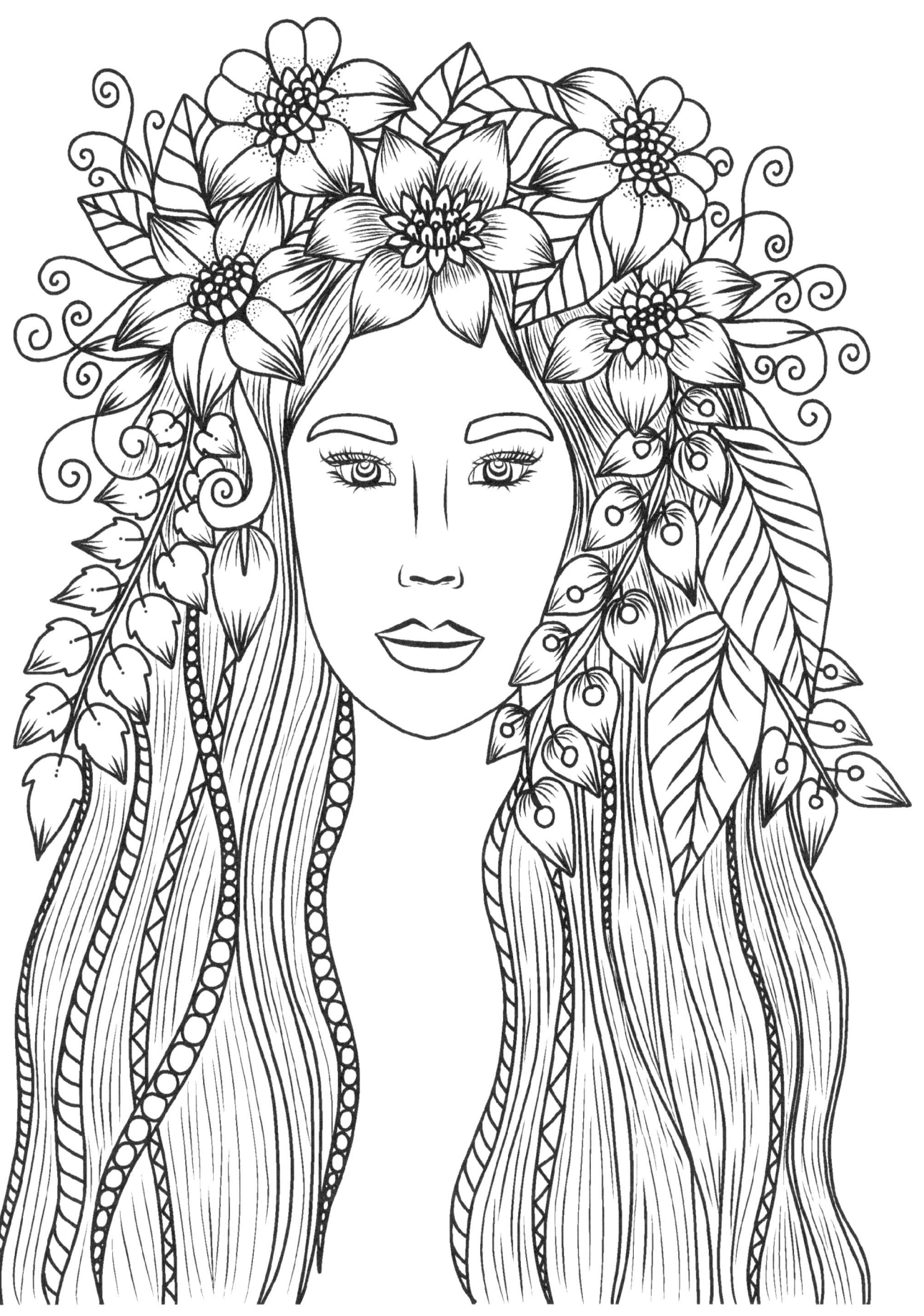

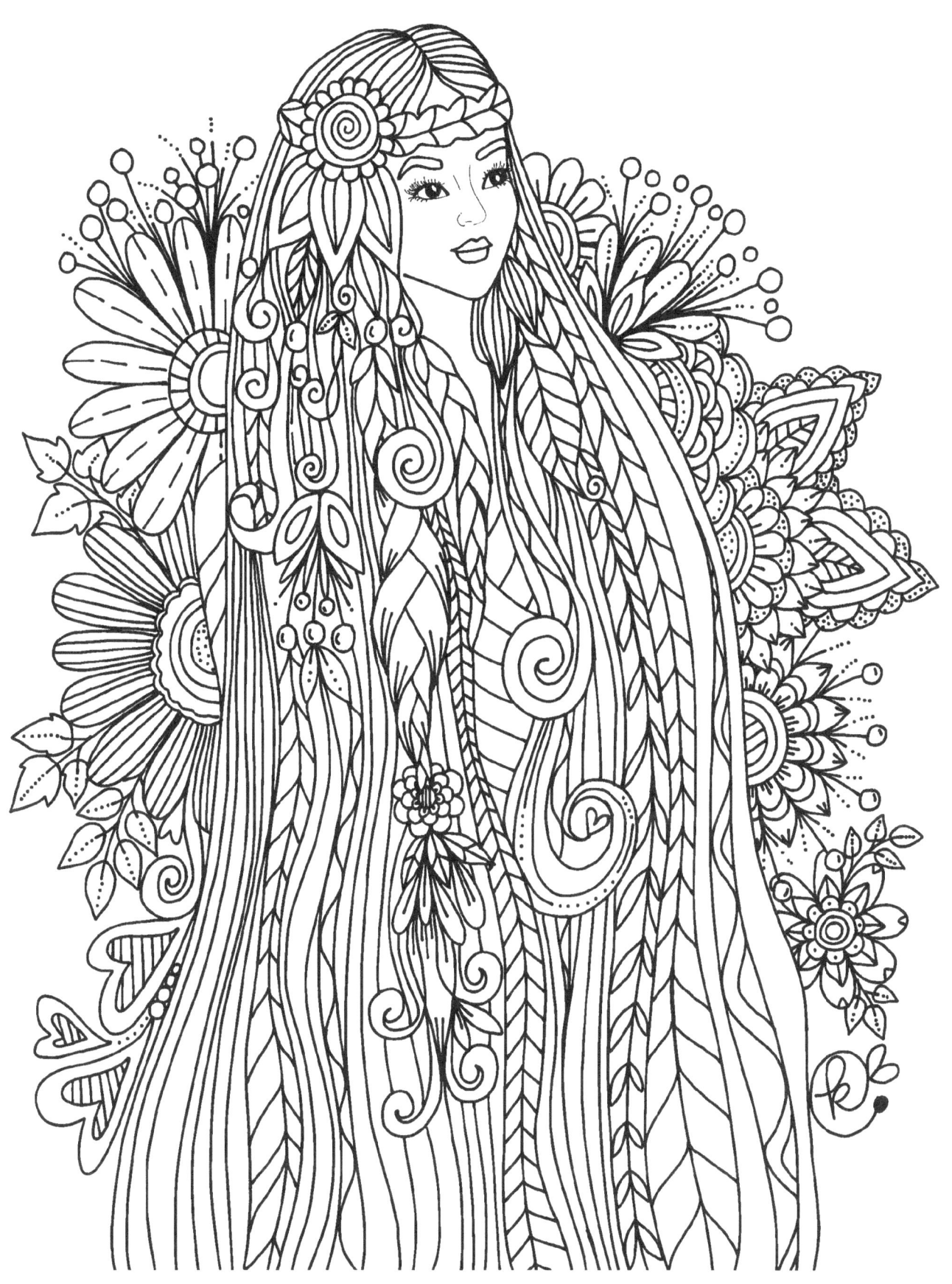

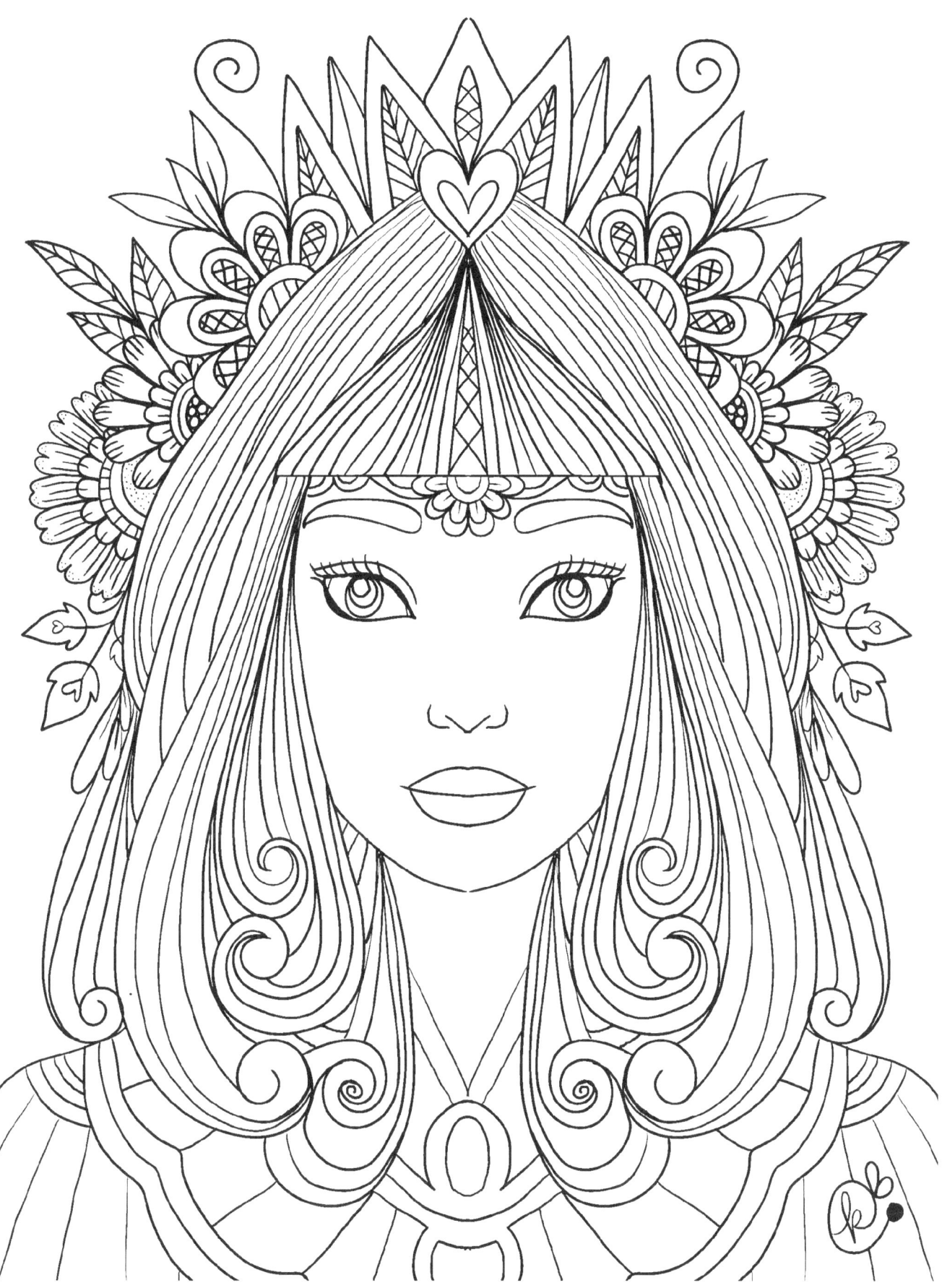

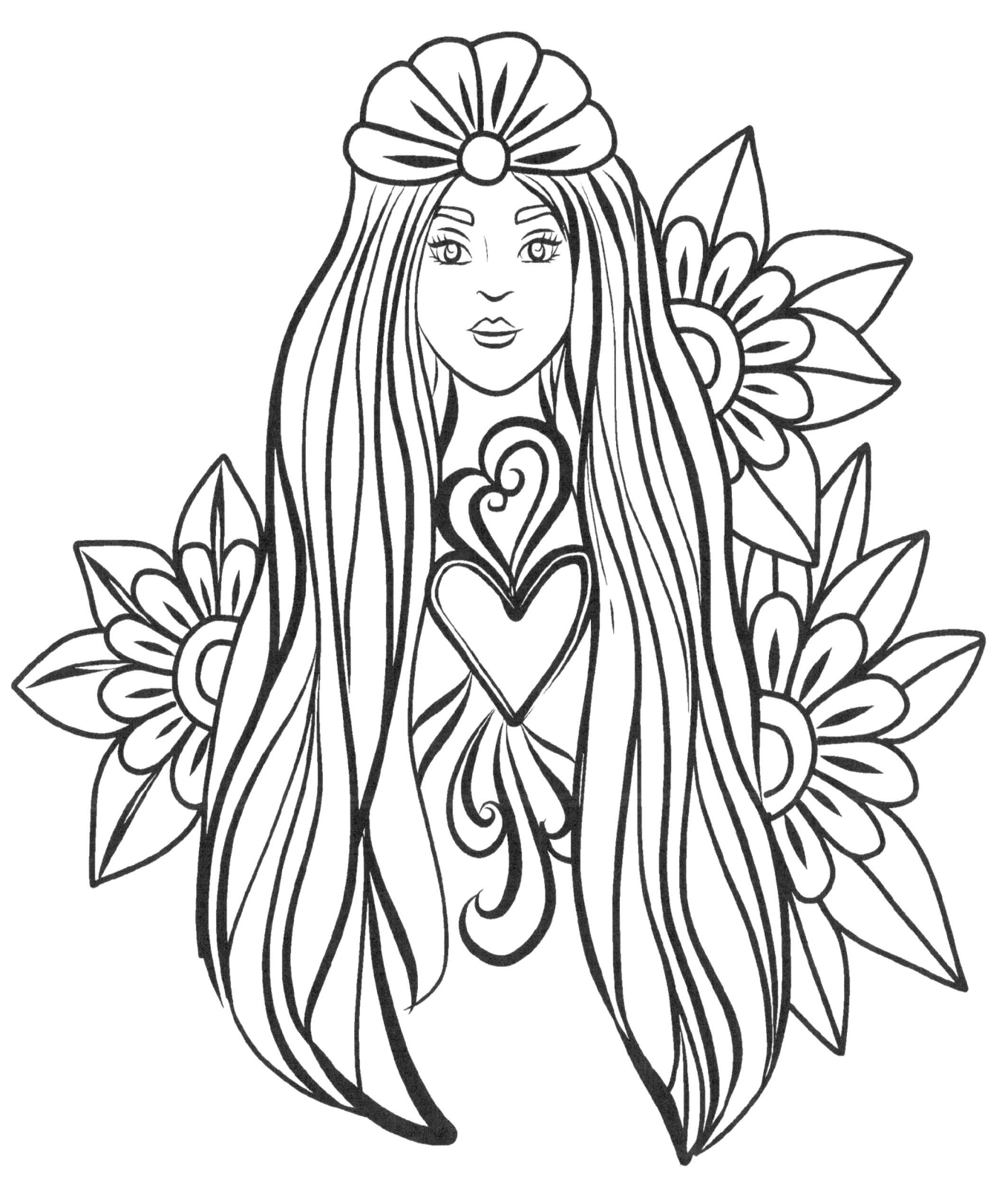

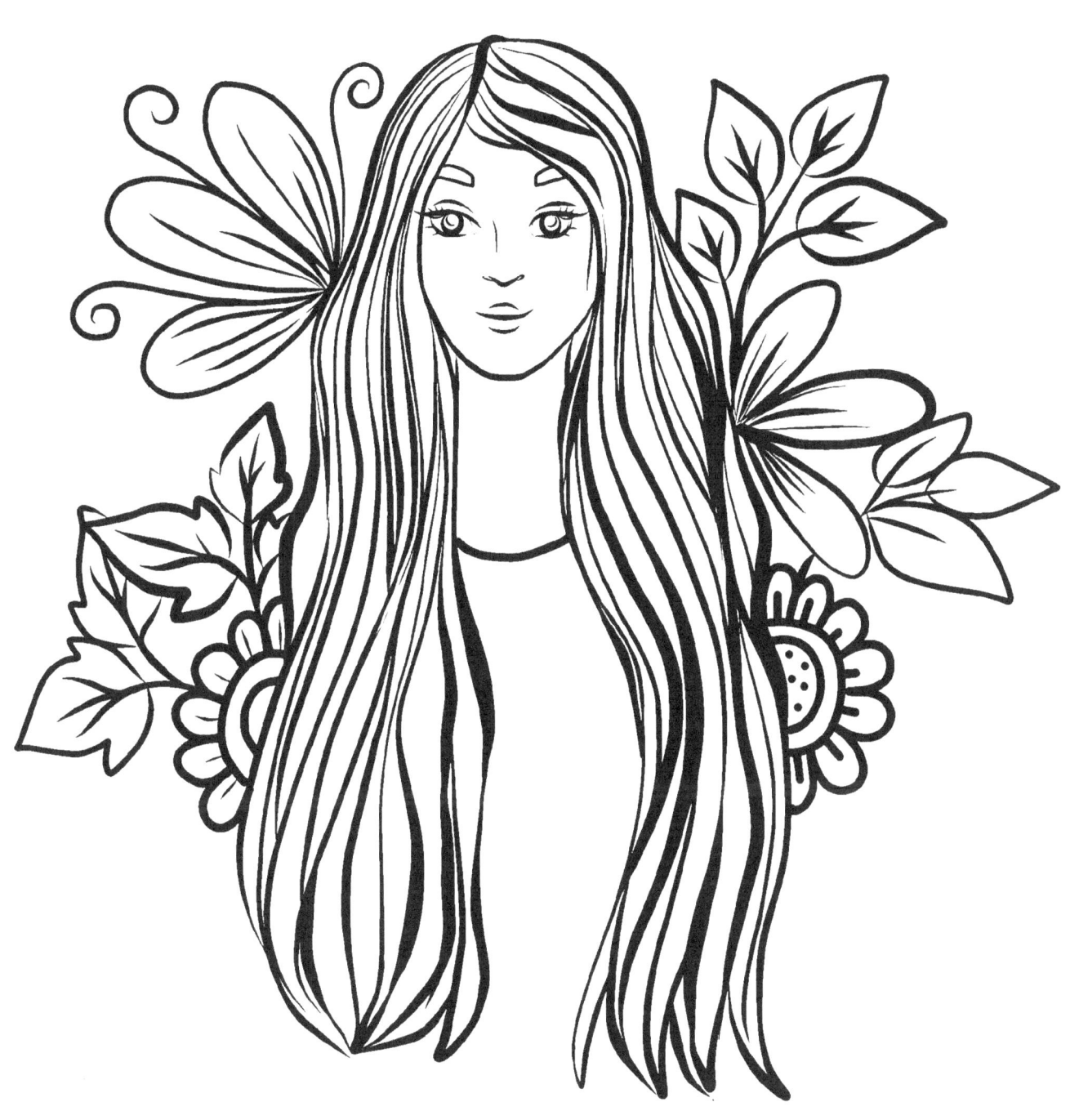

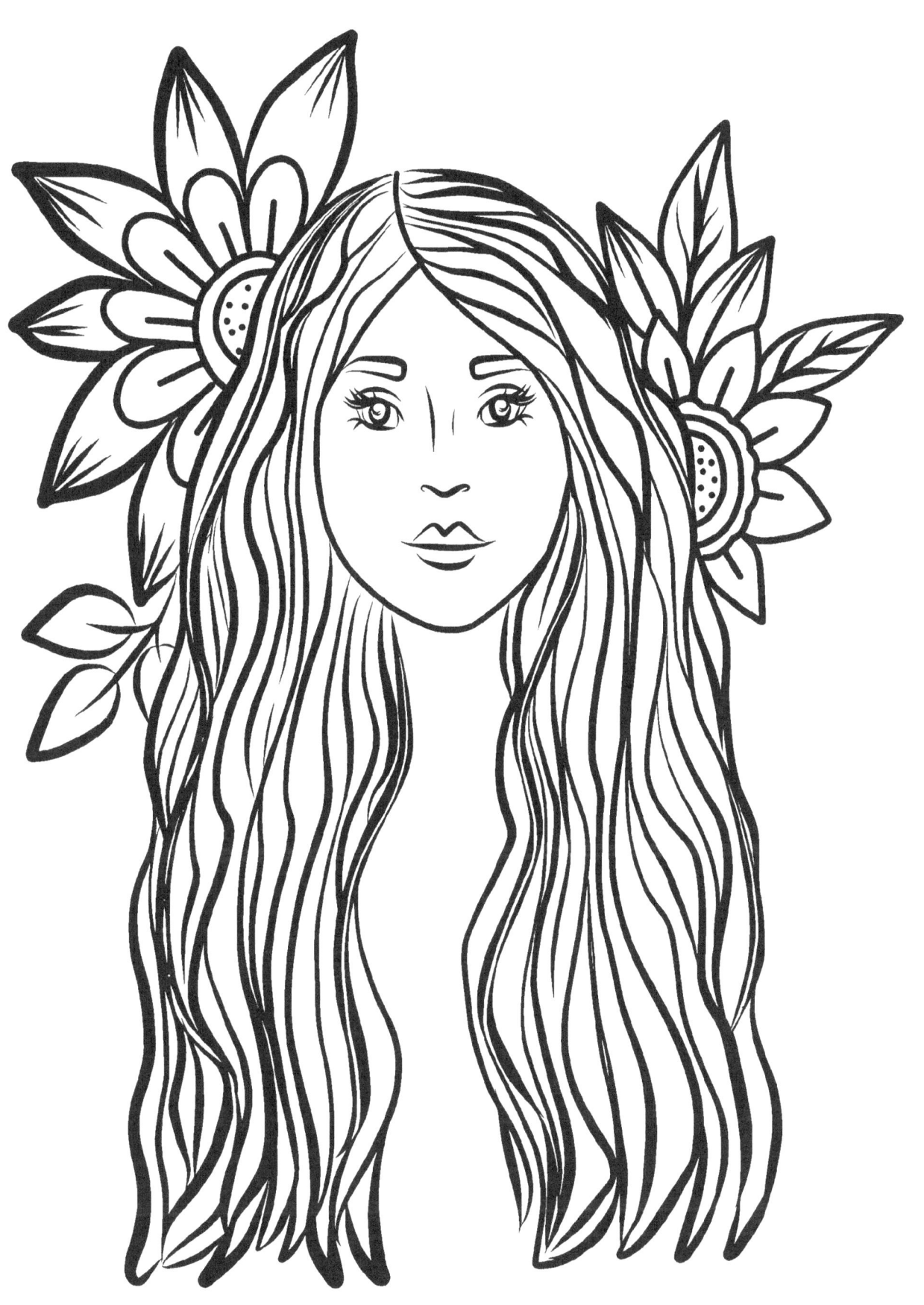

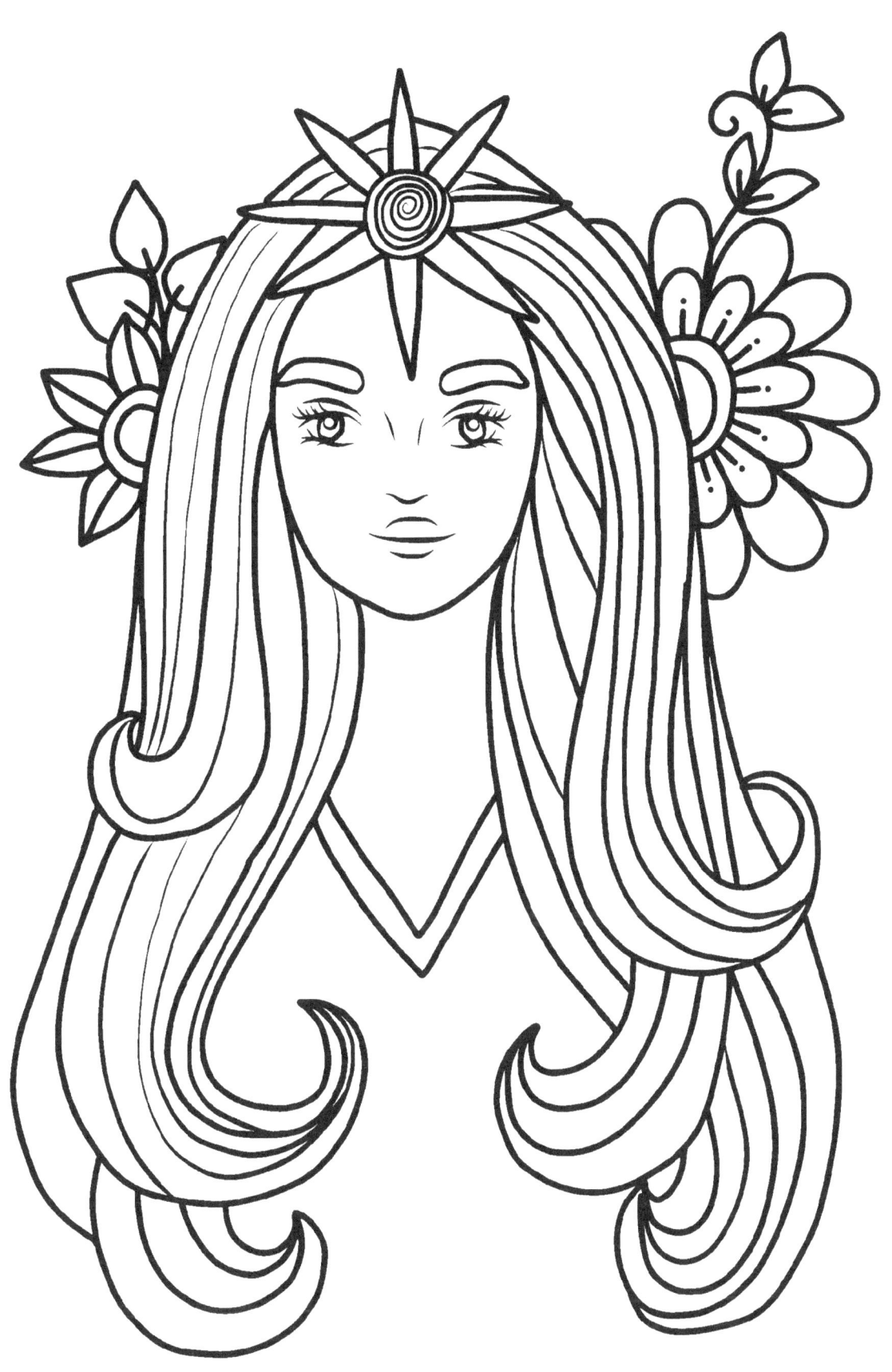

www.ingramcontent.com/pod-product-compliance
Lightning Source LLC
Chambersburg PA
CBHW082253220526
45469CB00009B/2988